CANADIAN GRAMMAR SPECTRUM

REFERENCE AND PRACTICE

George Yule

OXFORD

UNIVERSITY PRESS

OXFORD
UNIVERSITY PRESS

Oxford University Press is a department of the University of Oxford.

It furthers the University's objective of excellence in research, scholarship, and education by publishing worldwide. Oxford is a registered trade mark of Oxford University Press in the UK and in certain other countries.

Published in Canada by
Oxford University Press
8 Sampson Mews, Suite 204,
Don Mills, Ontario M3C 0H5 Canada

www.oupcanada.com

Library and Archives Canada Cataloguing in Publication
Yule, George. 1947–
Canadian grammar spectrum 7 : reference and practice / George Yule.

Includes index.
Previously published as part of: Yule, George.
Oxford practice grammar. Advanced, 2006.
ISBN 978-0-19-544836-8

1. English language—Grammar—Problems, exercises, etc.
2. English language—Textbooks for second language learners. I. Title.

PE1128.Y94 2012   428.2'4   C2011-903945-1

Credits

16 Quotation from *Oxford Guide to British and American Culture* published by Oxford University Press © Oxford University Press, 1999.

44 (Par. A) From "The Kid from Kogarah" from *Unreliable Memoirs* by Clive James published by Picador (Pan Books); (Par. D) From *That's Not What I Meant* by Deborah Tannen. Copyright © 1986 by Deborah Tannen; (Par. E) From *Libra* by Don DeLillo (Viking, 1988) copyright © Don DeLillo, 1988.

60 Adapted from "Saying what's hard to say" by Sara Shandler published in *Seventeen Magazine*.

85 Adapteded from *I Can't Accept Not Trying* by Michael Jordan. Copyright © 1994 by Rare Air, Ltd. Text © 1994 by Michael Jordan.

Illustrations: page 16 by Adrian Barclay, page 83 by Donna Guilfoyle/ArtPlus Ltd.

Contents

Pronouns

Adjectives and adverbs

Prepositions

Infinitives and gerunds

Reported speech

Noun clauses

Relative clauses

Conditionals

Adverbial clauses

Connectors and focus structures

Review test

Appendix: Regular and irregular verbs

Glossary

Answer key

Index

Introduction

Canadian Grammar Spectrum is a series of books, each written at the appropriate level for you at each stage in your study of English. The series is intended for your use either in a classroom or when working independently on your own time.

The books are divided into two- to four-page units, each of which covers an important grammar topic. Each unit starts with an explanation of the grammar and this is followed by a set of practice exercises. A test at the end of each book gives the opportunity for more practice and enables you to assess how much you have learned. Answers to the exercises and the test are provided at the back of the book.

You may want to choose the order in which you study the grammar topics, perhaps going first to those giving you problems. (Topics are listed in the Contents page at the front of each book and in the Index at the back.) Alternatively, you may choose to start at the beginning of each book and work through to the end.

The emphasis throughout this book is on the meaning and use of the grammatical forms. The explanations of grammar are descriptions of how English works; they are a guide to help you understand, not rules to be memorized. It is often more effective to look at examples of English rather than to read statements about it, and the grammar explanations are supported by lots of examples of everyday conversational English.

Key to symbols

The symbol / (oblique stroke) between two words means that either word is possible. *I may/might go* means that *I may go* and *I might go* are both possible. In exercise questions this symbol is also used to separate words or phrases which are possible answers.

Parentheses ( ) around a word or phrase in the middle of a sentence mean that it can be left out. *There's (some) milk in the fridge* means that there are two possible sentences: *There's some milk in the fridge* and *There's milk in the fridge*.

The symbol ~ means that there is a change of speaker. In the example *How are you? ~ I'm fine, thanks*, the question and answer are spoken by different people.

The symbol ▶ in an exercise indicates that a sample answer is given.

Sentences

We can form simple sentences with a subject and a verb in a single clause (*Jenny laughed*). We can include auxiliary verbs (**be, do, have**, and modals) as part of the verb phrase and an adverbial after the verb (*She was sitting at the table*). We can use verbs with an object (*She was drawing a picture*), without an object (*She giggled*), or with two objects (*She showed me the picture*). We can also use linking verbs with complements (*It looked very silly*).

We form compound sentences with clauses joined by the coordinating conjunctions **and, but**, and **or** (*I made some coffee, but Jenny wanted orange juice*). We form complex sentences with clauses joined by subordinating conjunctions such as **after, because, if**, and **while** (*We talked in the kitchen while I made breakfast*).

A Read through this newspaper report and find

1 a simple sentence
2 a complex sentence with two conjunctions

A 16-YEAR-OLD SASKATCHEWAN boy will receive a Medal for Bravery, after rescuing a young girl who had fallen through thin ice on Wascana Lake.
5 Last Saturday, Nolan Agecoutay, of Regina, was walking through Wascana Park with some friends when he heard cries for help. He and his friends quickly realized that the yelling was coming from the ice. A group of
10 four young teenagers had been playing hockey when the ice cracked and one 12-year-old girl fell into the icy water.

Agecoutay ran to the scene of the accident. He dropped onto his stomach and crawled to
15 the hole in the ice where the girl was struggling. He grabbed one of the hockey sticks lying on the ice and used it to reach out to the victim. He admits that it was a scary situation, but said "I tried to remain calm
20 when I was talking to her. I knew that if she stopped panicking and grabbed the end of the stick, I would be able to pull her out."

After Agecoutay had pulled the girl to safety, he wrapped her in his own jacket
25 while they waited for an ambulance, which showed up a few minutes later. Emergency responders called the teenager a hero. They said that he had done the right thing crawling onto the ice instead of walking, and
30 praised him for staying calm. Agecoutay credits his grandfather for teaching him proper survival skills. He said "I didn't even have to think about what I was doing. I saw that someone needed help and I knew that
35 I had to do something."

The City of Regina would like to remind everyone to stay off the ice until officials announce that it is safe for skating. The group of young teenagers took an enormous
40 risk when they ignored the signs posted around the lake. Luckily for one little girl, Nolan Agecoutay was there to prevent a tragedy. ■

B Using verbs and conjunctions from the newspaper report above, complete this summary.

Teenager Nolan Agecoutay (▶) .....pulled..... a girl to safety (1) ...After..... she (2) ...fell....... through the ice on Wascana Lake. He dropped to his stomach (3) ...and..... crawled across the ice to her. He then used a hockey stick to (4) ...pull..... her out of the water. (5) ...After..... rescuing her, he (6) ...wrapped... her in his jacket to keep her warm. (7) ...Because... of his actions, Agecoutay will receive a Medal for Bravery.

Simple sentences

A simple sentence is a single clause with a subject and a verb.

    1 *Gisella sneezed.* • *Somebody coughed.* • *The bus didn't come.* • *People were waiting.*

Simple sentences can also have an object (2) and/or an adverbial, such as an adverb (3) or a prepositional phrase (4).

    2 *Mr. Rampaul made **lunch**.* • *I brought **some cookies**.* • *We drank **coffee**.* • *Everyone enjoyed **it**.*
    3 ***Suddenly** the weather changed.* • *We **quickly** closed the windows.* • *It **often** rains **there**.*
    4 *Shakespeare married Anne Hathaway **in 1582**. He moved **to London in 1588**.*

Simple sentences with linking verbs, such as **be** or **look**, have complements that describe the subject.

    5 *Frank is **a nurse**.* • *He wasn't **ready**.* • *His hair looked **wet**.* • *The room felt **like an oven**.*

Verbs

Most verbs are action verbs, used to describe actions (what we do) and events (what happens).

    6 *Richard **eats** a lot of pasta. It **gives** him energy. He **runs** every night. I **saw** him in the park.*

Some verbs are stative verbs rather than action verbs. They are used to describe states: what we think (7), how we feel (8), and relationships, especially those concerned with inclusion and possession (9).

    7 *I **know** what you **mean**.* • *My parents **understood** everything.* • *They **believe** in fate.*
    8 *I **appreciate** all your help.* • *Some people **hate** mustard on sandwiches.*
    9 *The city guide **contains** useful information.* • *That old suitcase **belongs** to me.*
We don't usually use stative verbs in the progressive. (NOT ~~That suitcase is belonging to me.~~)
Other stative verbs include **consist of, exist, include, matter, own, prefer, realize, remember, resemble**

We also use linking verbs (**be, seem**, etc.) to describe states: how things are or seem to be.

    10 *These flowers **are** beautiful.* • *Everything **seems** fine.* • *Your friend **appears** to be nervous.*

We can use some verbs, such as **taste** or **weigh**, as stative verbs (11) or as action verbs (12).

    11 *Flowers don't usually **taste** very good.* • *The box **weighs** two kilograms.*
    12 *Have you **tasted** this soup?* • *They **weighed** it at the post office.*

We use the auxiliary verbs **be, do**, and **have** with other verbs when we form different tenses (13), in questions and negatives (14), and for emphasis (15).

    13 *The boys **have been** waiting for you. I think they**'ve** gone outside. They**'re** playing soccer.*
    14 *What **did** Josh say? ~ He **didn't** say anything.* • ***Does** he want coffee? ~ I **don't** think so.*
    15 *You aren't working very hard. ~ I **am** working hard!* • *You don't miss me. ~ I **do** miss you!*
We also use **be, do**, and **have** as main verbs: *He **is** lazy. He **does** nothing. He **has** no money.*

We use modal auxiliary verbs (modals) such as **can, must, should**, or **will** with other verbs to express concepts such as permission, obligation, necessity, prediction, etc.

    16 ***Can** I leave now?* • *You **shouldn't** go yet.* • *I **must** catch the next bus or I**'ll** be late for work.*

Subjects and verbs

Subjects

The subject of a sentence is usually the first noun phrase or pronoun identifying who or what is performing an action expressed by the verb (1). It can identify who or what is experiencing something (2). It can also be the focus of a description (i.e. who or what the complement is linked to) (3).

1 ***Tony** lost his keys.* • ***The dog** ate my homework.* • ***You** are working too hard these days.*
2 ***The children** heard a loud noise.* • ***The audience** enjoyed the concert.* • ***Meg** doesn't like coffee.*
3 ***Moose** are large and powerful.* • ***Her new classmates** seem friendly.* • ***Your hair** looks great.*

We usually put the subject before the verb except in questions (4) and sentences using inversion (5).

4 *Where has **she** been?* • *Does **this bus** go to the university?* • *Isn't **Lunenburg** in Nova Scotia?*
5 *In front of us and blocking the way stood **a large dog**. Never had **I** seen such a fierce animal.*

The subject can also be a gerund (6), an infinitive (7), or a clause (8).

6 ***Reading books** is her favourite thing.* • ***Studying** always makes me sleepy.*
7 ***Just to complete the classes** has become my new goal.* • ***To go without you** wouldn't be any fun.*
8 ***That the NDP would win the election** was never in doubt.* • ***What he said** wasn't very polite.*

Subject-verb agreement

The subject determines whether the verb is singular or plural (9). It is the main noun or subject, not a prepositional phrase, that makes the verb singular (10) or plural (11).

9 *Asad's **sister lives** in Montreal. His **parents live** near Calgary.*
10 *A new pair of shoes **doesn't** cost a lot.* • *A woman with three children **was** waiting outside.*
11 *New shoes **don't** always feel comfortable at first.* • *The children **were** crying.*

We use singular verbs after indefinite pronouns (**everybody**, **nobody**, etc.) as subjects (12). We usually use singular verbs after subjects beginning with **none of** and **neither of** (13). We sometimes use plural verbs in informal situations (14).

12 *Everybody in the country **wants** one of these.* • *Nobody except his parents **was** willing to help.*
13 *None of the candidates **has** much support.* • *Neither of them **was** skating very well.*
14 *She shouted, "None of you **have** a chance."* • *He's complaining that neither of them **were** asked.*

We use singular verbs after some subjects that seem to be plural: some nouns ending in **-s** (15), phrases describing an amount (16), and some combinations with **and** (17). There are some nouns such as **people** and **police** that appear to be singular, but that are used with a plural verb (18).

15 *The news **wasn't** too bad.* • *Measles **is** a disease.*
16 *Fifty dollars **is** too much.* • *Twenty kilometres **was** too far and two days **wasn't** enough time.*
17 *Tom and Jerry **is** a violent cartoon.* • *Rice and beans **doesn't** cost very much.*
18 *The police **are** trying to stop speeding in the city, but people **are** still driving too fast.*

We usually use a group noun to refer to the group as a single unit, with a singular verb.

19 *Our team **is** in second place.* • *The committee **hasn't** reached a decision yet.*
Other group nouns include **audience, class, crowd, enemy, family, government, orchestra, staff**

A Add one of these verbs to each of the sentences.

~~does~~, doesn't, has, have, is, isn't, are, aren't, was, wasn't, won't

▶ Excuse me, but *does* this bus stop in Waterloo?

1 To get an A in every class *won't* be easy.

2 *Lord of the Flies* the name of the book we *have* had to read last year?

3 My new pair of jeans *has* pockets on the side of the legs.

4 What they're doing in Parliament *is* interest me.

5 Being absent from class a lot going to improve his chances of passing.

6 Jan got really angry with us and screamed, "None of you *are* my friends anymore!"

7 Never I had to listen to so many boring people!

8 I watched *Dances with Wolves*, which about dancing at all.

9 *was* Statistics more difficult than Economics?

10 These new sunglasses *aren't* made of glass or plastic or anything like that.

B Choose an ending (a–e) for each beginning (1–5) and add an appropriate form of the verb *be*.

▶ *The Simpsons* ..... is ..... (f.)
1 *Romeo and Juliet* ..... ~~are~~ is (C.)
2 Last night's news ... are .... (e.)
3 Twenty-five kilograms ... are ... (a.)
4 Juan and all his friends ... are ... (d.)
5 The audience .... is .... (b.)

a a lot to carry by yourself, don't you think?
b usually seated before the play starts.
c written by Shakespeare.
d going camping this weekend.
e very interesting, I thought.
f the name of a TV show.

C Complete each sentence with one of these words plus *has* or *have*.

committee, marbles, ~~diabetes~~, eggs, everybody, nobody, orchestra, police, teachers

▶ Diabetes has become a more common disease, mainly because of the way we eat.

1 The conductor and the .... had very little time to rehearse for the concert.

2 Security is just something that .... to go through in airports nowadays.

3 .... from the new student group .... volunteered to help with the year-end party.

4 Members of the planning .... all been given individual copies of the agenda for the meeting.

5 .... always been a popular game for children.

6 According to the rules, none of the .... the right to make students stay after school.

7 The .... no idea how the robbers got into the bank.

8 Bacon and .... been the Sunday breakfast in our house for years.

Verbs and objects

Verbs with objects (transitive verbs)

Transitive verbs have objects—usually noun phrases or pronouns.

   1   *He **kicked** a small stone. It **hit** me. • We **discussed** the problems. They **affected** all of us.*

We use a transitive verb to describe an action that affects an object (2) or to describe a feeling or experience caused by an object (3).

   2   *Are they **building** a wall? • I'll **cut** the grass. • Kerwood **bought** an old Volkswagen.*
Others include **carry, catch, fix, heat, prepare, protect, rob, scratch, sell, trim**

   3   *Did you **enjoy** the concert? • One of our old teachers **remembered** us. • I don't **like** onions.*
Others include **admire, believe, fear, hate, hear, love, need, please, prefer, receive**

Only transitive verbs can be used in the passive.

   4   *Someone **stole** my bag.* → *My bag was stolen. • They **caught** the thief.* → *The thief was caught.*

We usually use a prepositional phrase after the object of a transitive verb such as **put**.

   5   *He **put** the keys <u>in the drawer</u>. • We **crammed** all our boxes <u>into the back of Kara's car</u>.*

Verbs without objects (intransitive verbs)

Intransitive verbs are used without an object.

   6   *I can't **sleep**. • Everyone was **waiting**, but he didn't **care**.* (NOT ~~He didn't care it.~~)
Others include **arrive, depart, disappear, happen, hesitate, occur, pause, rain**

We use intransitive verbs when we refer to simple events, actions, and sounds.

   7   *The roof **collapsed**. • She **sighed** and **yawned**. • A lot of people **were screaming**.*
Others include **cough, faint, fall, growl, moan, scream, shiver, sneeze**

Intransitive verbs are not used in the passive.

   8   *The thief **escaped**.* (NOT ~~The thief was escaped. The police were escaped by the thief.~~)

We often use prepositional phrases after intransitive verbs (9), especially verbs describing movement (10).

   9   *Darwin **died** in 1882. • I **slept** until noon. • He is **sleeping** on the couch and **snoring**.*

  10   *It **came** from Argentina. • Let's **go** to bed. • We **walk** to the park and then we **run** around it.*

Verbs used with and without objects

We can use some verbs, such as **eat** or **read**, with objects (11) or without objects (12).

  11   *She **read** his note. • I don't **eat** fish. • We **won** the game. • Do you **speak** English?*

  12   *He always **reads** when he's **eating**. • Did you **win**? • She was so upset she couldn't **speak**.*
Others include **cook, draw, dress, drink, drive, hurt, paint, spread, study, write**

There are some verbs, such as **die** or **smile**, that we usually use without an object (13), but that can also be used with one particular object (14).

  13   *Ariana **smiled** and said she was quite certain that none of us would ever **die**.*

  14   *Nina **smiled** her bright smile. She seemed unconcerned that she might **die** a painful death.*
Others include **dance, dream, laugh, live, sigh**

We can use some verbs, such as **fight** or **meet**, with objects (15). We can also use them without objects after plural subjects when **each other** (16) or **with each other** (17) is understood.

  15   *When I **met** Sergio in San Jose, he **embraced** me like a brother. • Gianni had to **fight** two muggers.*

  16   *We **met** in Rome. • Our fingers **touched**. • The old women **embraced**. • They **hugged** and **kissed**.*

  17   *Gianni and I always **fight**. • Two of the Okanagan Valley's major wine producers **have merged**.*

A Using a dictionary if necessary, complete these definitions with the nouns and appropriate forms of the verbs. Add the word *things* after any verb that needs an object.

hallucination	hinge		
~~hassle~~	suitcase		
hijacker	hypocrite		

behave	close	go	seize
carry	demand	pretend	swing
~~cause~~	~~do~~	see	travel

(▶) A .... *hassle* .... is something that is annoying because it .... *causes* .... problems or difficulties when you try to ... *do things* ....

A (1) .... is a large case in which you can (2) .... when you (3) ....

A (4) .... is a small piece of metal on which a door (5) .... as it opens and (6) ....

A (7) .... is a feeling or belief that you are (8) .... when nothing is there.

A (9) .... is a person who (10) .... to have high values that are not matched by the way he or she (11) ....

A (12) .... is a person who (13) .... control of a vehicle, especially an airplane, in order to (14) .... to a new destination or to (15) .... from a government in return for the safety of those in the vehicle.

B Choose an answer (a–d) for each question (1–4) and add appropriate forms of these verbs. If necessary, add the pronoun *it* and/or a preposition.

believe, go, hear, like, put, shiver, take, wait

1 Did Andreas .... the key? (...)
2 Do you .... big cities? (...)
3 Could you .... outside? (...)
4 Have you .... the latest rumour? (...)

a Yes, but I don't ....
b Yes, he .... his pocket.
c Yes, that's why I'm .... Toronto.
d No, it's too cold and I'm ....

C Add the correct pair of intransitive verbs to each sentence. Use appropriate forms.

breathe / snore	~~dream / sleep~~	eat / hibernate	fall / lie
get / move	go / sing	happen / talk	nap / rest

▶ When you .... *dream* .... , you see and experience things while you are ... *sleeping* ..... .

1 Someone who .... up and .... around while asleep is called a sleepwalker.

2 When people in hot countries .... or .... after lunch, it's called having a siesta.

3 Animals that .... don't .... at all while they spend the winter in a deep sleep.

4 When you .... awake at night and you can't .... asleep, you have insomnia.

5 If someone .... about a place as "sleepy," it means that nothing much .... there.

6 When you .... softly to help a child .... to sleep, you are singing a lullaby.

7 People who .... very noisily when they are sleeping.

Verbs with indirect objects and clauses

Verbs with indirect objects

We use two objects after some verbs: an indirect object and a direct object. With a verb such as **send**, we can put the indirect object after the verb (1) or after the preposition **to** (2). The indirect object (**you, Joe, everyone**) receives the direct object (**postcard, note, form**).

    1 *I'll send* ***you*** *a postcard.* • *She handed* ***Joe*** *the note.* • *Did you give* ***everyone*** *a form?*

    2 *I'll send a postcard* ***to you.*** • *She handed the note* ***to Joe.*** • *Did you give a form* ***to everyone?***

Others include **bring, lend, mail, offer, pass, read, sell, show, teach, tell, throw, write**

We don't put **to** + indirect object before a direct object (NOT *Did you give to everyone a form?*).

With a verb such as **buy**, we can put the indirect object after the verb (3) or after the preposition **for** (4). The indirect object (**him, me, you**) benefits from the action of the verb (*buy, do, make*).

    3 *She bought* ***him*** *a tie.* • *Can you do* ***me*** *a favour?* • *I'll make* ***you*** *a sandwich.*

    4 *She bought a tie* ***for him.*** • *Can you do a favour* ***for me?*** • *I'll make a sandwich* ***for you.***

Others include **build, cook, cut, draw, find, get, keep, leave, order, pick, save**

We don't put **for** + indirect object before a direct object (NOT *I'll make for you a sandwich.*)

We put shorter objects, especially pronouns, before longer objects (5). When we use pronouns for both objects after the verb, we put the indirect object pronoun first (6).

    5 *Show* ***me*** *the prize you won.* • *Show* ***it*** *to everyone who said you couldn't do it.* • *Show* ***it*** *to them!*

    6 *Show* ***me*** *it.* (NOT *Show it me.*) • *I'll make* ***you*** *one.* (NOT *I'll make one you.*)

With verbs such as **describe** or **explain**, we put the indirect object after a preposition, not after the verb. But compare (14) below.

    7 *He described the man* ***to them.*** • *He explained the plan* ***to us.*** (NOT *He explained us the plan.*)

Others include **admit, announce, mention, murmur, report, shout, suggest, whisper**

Note that these are often verbs of speaking: *He said "Hello"* ***to me.*** (NOT *He said me "Hello."*)

With a verb such as **cost**, we must put the indirect object after the verb.

    8 *The mistake cost* ***us*** *a lot of money.* • *They fined* ***him*** *$250.* • *I bet* ***you*** *$5.* (NOT *I bet $5 to you.*)

Others include **deny, forgive, refuse**

Verbs with clauses

We can use **that**-clauses as direct objects after "thinking" verbs such as **believe** or **think** (9) and after "reporting" verbs such as **explain** or **say** (10).

    9 *They believed* ***that*** *the sun went around the earth.* • *He thinks* **that** *the students are lazy.*

    10 *She said* ***that*** *she would be late.* • *He explained* ***that*** *there was no money left.*

Note that the word **that** is often omitted: *He thinks the students are lazy.*

After verbs reporting questions, we can begin the clause with **if, whether** (11), or a **wh**-word (12).

    11 *The teacher asked* ***if*** *anyone was absent.* • *They enquired* ***whether*** *it was legal or not.*

    12 *We should ask* ***what*** *it costs.* • *I wonder* ***when*** *they'll make the decision.*

After reporting verbs such as **remind** or **tell**, we must have an indirect object before the clause.

    13 *I'll remind* ***him*** *that you're here.* • *You told* ***me*** *that he was sick.* (NOT *You told that he was sick.*)

Others include **assure, convince, inform, notify**

After a reporting verb such as **admit**, we must use **to** before an indirect object before a clause.

    14 *He admitted* ***to the police*** *that he had stolen the money.* (NOT *He admitted the police that he had stolen the money.*)

    She mentioned ***to me*** *that she hated her job.* (NOT *She mentioned me that she hated her job.*)

Others include **boast, confess, declare, hint, propose, reveal**

A Complete each sentence in such a way that it is as similar as possible in meaning to the sentence or sentences before it.

▶ They had it. Now we have it. They gave ...it to us...

1 She quietly wished him good luck.
   She whispered ....

2 She was ordered by the judge to pay $500 for her actions.
   The judge fined ....

3 The farmer wouldn't give permission to us to walk across his field.
   The farmer refused ....

4 Juan took Caroline's book. He told me.
   Juan confessed ....

B Using a dictionary if necessary, complete the sentences with appropriate forms of these verbs. Add appropriate pronouns and prepositions if necessary.

find, offer, reserve, sell, spread, transmit, keep, require, retrieve, ~~send~~, trade, ~~transport~~

▶ Your boxes will be ...transported... by air. We will ...send them to... you soon.

1 In a restaurant, if a table is ...., that means the restaurant is .... a special person or group.

2 Contagious diseases are easily .... People with contagious diseases can easily .... the rest of the population.

3 Those computer files that I thought I had lost were .... by Sotiris. I was so glad that he .... me.

4 In baseball, when a player is ...., it means that one team .... another team.

5 In a university, if certain courses are ...., it means that all students must take those courses and the university must .... students every year.

C Correct the mistakes in this text.

During the psychology class, one student reported ~~us~~ her experiment ^to us /She explained us that it was about communication between husbands and wives. The researcher gave the following information half of the husbands. "Your wife has described you a trip to China. One of her friends told to her about it. You think sounds like a really good idea, so you ask to her some questions about the cost." The other group of husbands heard the following information. "Your wife has suggested you a trip to China. You don't like. You believe is a really bad idea, so you ask some questions her about the cost." The researcher didn't tell to the wives she said to the husbands. She asked the wives to listen to the tape recording of their husbands' questions and decide the husbands thought it was a good idea or not. A significant number of the wives couldn't decide. That was very surprising.

Tenses

Tense is the relationship between the form of the verb and the time of the action or state it describes. We often use the auxiliary verbs **be** and **have** with other verbs when we form different tenses. See page 11 for a table of English verb forms and tenses.

A Read through this text and find

1 another sentence with *be* as a main verb
2 a sentence with *be* and a sentence with *have* as auxiliary verbs

A │This October 31st is a scary day for Dylan Barnes, not just because it is Halloween, but because it is a special anniversary for him.│ For several years he will have been trying to turn a good idea into a successful business via the Internet. He won't be doing anything special to celebrate the occasion, mainly because his business venture won't have made any money for most of the past year. Like his two business partners before him, he will soon need to do something else.

B   When they started, it had seemed like such a great idea. Dylan and his friend, Michael Underwood, had been writing up their lecture notes as complete sets, with review sheets and sample tests, and selling them to other students. They had used that money to pay for complete sets of notes from other big lecture classes, which they then sold to an eager population of new students. They were starting to make a small steady profit when they met Terry Lloyd. Terry had been creating home pages for his friends, then larger websites on the Internet, and he showed them how to do it too. Using the initials of their last names, they created Bullnotes, established a website, and set out to become entrepreneurs of the information age.

C   They soon found that students were looking for more than lecture notes. They needed to do other things that they weren't learning in their classes. Imagine that you are applying for a scholarship. You have been trying to write a letter of application and you can't get it right. You need an example of the kind of letter you are trying to write. Or maybe someone has asked you to write a letter of recommendation. From the

---

. . . everyone wants these things, but no one wants to pay for them.

---

website you could download the basic form of the letter with spaces in it for your own details. "I am writing this letter in support of . . . . whom I have known for . . . . years," and so on.

D   Soon there were all kinds of forms available from Bullnotes, from passport application forms to those for making a will. Dylan was working day and night to make the material available, but he didn't think about what he was doing in terms of a business. The big problem, they soon discovered, is that everyone wants these things, but no one wants to pay for them. In what turned out to be a common experience for many people who tried to create Internet businesses, they had a successful website, but they didn't really make any money from it.

E   Terry quickly found a highly paid job with an investment company and Michael went off to work for a software manufacturer. Dylan is still looking for a way to make Bullnotes work as a business, but these days he is always counting his pennies and he is having a hard time paying his bills. He has thought about taking a teaching job after seeing an ad for a teacher of business writing with business experience. He has lots of experience now and there really won't be a problem with the letter of application.

B Choose one of the following as the final sentence of each of the paragraphs (A–E) above.

1 They were ready to become millionaires. . . .
2 He also knows where to find some good lecture notes. . . .
3 Everyone acted as if the information was free. . . .
4 He will have to find a job. . . .
5 Writing was a couple of clicks, then a fill-in-the-blanks exercise. . . .

Verbs, auxiliary verbs, and tenses

The base form of the verb is listed in the dictionary. It is used in the imperative and the infinitive.
> 1 **Stop!** • *Please **wait**.* • *Don't **be** impatient.* • ***Ask** someone to **help** you.* • *Let's **try** to **find** a solution.*

The base form is also called the bare infinitive or the infinitive without **to**.

Most verbs are used to describe actions or events (2). Some verbs are used for states (3).
> 2 *Do you **play** chess?* • *I'll **open** a window.* • *Someone has **taken** my book.* • *The crowd is **cheering**.*
> 3 *Do you **know** Marc?* • *Anil **seems** really nice.* • *Her parents **own** a roti shop.* • *I **believe** you.*

We don't usually use stative verbs in the progressive form. (NOT ~~I'm believing you.~~)

We use the auxiliary **do** with the base form to make questions and negatives in the Simple Present and Simple Past.
> 4 *What **did** Khalida **want** for lunch?* ~ *She **didn't want** anything.* • ***Does** she **feel** better?* ~ *I **don't know**.*

We use the auxiliary **be** with the present participle (**-ing** form) of the verb to make progressive forms (5) and the auxiliary **have** with the past participle (**-ed**) to make perfect forms (6). We use auxiliary **have** + **been** with the present participle to make perfect progressive forms (7).
> 5 ***Are** you **waiting** for me?* • *Shea **isn't using** his computer.* • *They **were working** all night.*
> 6 ***Have** you **finished** already?* • *The mail **hasn't come** yet.* • *Andy **had forgotten** to bring the keys.*
> 7 ***Have** you **been sleeping**?* • *It **hasn't been snowing** recently.* • *We **had been studying** for hours.*

We use modal auxiliaries (modals) with the base form of the verb or with the auxiliaries **be** and **have**.
> 8 *They **will help** us.* • *I'll **be waiting** for you.* • *We **won't have finished**.* (NOT ~~We won't finished.~~)

C Complete this table with one example of each form from the text on page 10.

Imperative or infinitive: base form	*play*
Simple Present: base form or base form + **s** in third person singular	*play* *plays*
Present Progressive: present **be** + present participle	*am/is/are playing*
Present Perfect: present **have** + past participle	*has/have played*
Present Perfect Progressive: present **have** + **been** + present participle	*has/have been playing*
Simple Past: base form + **ed** (or irregular form)	*played*
Past Progressive: past **be** + present participle	*was/were playing*
Past Perfect: past **have** + past participle	*had played*
Past Perfect Progressive: past **have** + **been** + present participle	*had been playing*
Future: **will** + base form	*will play*
Future Progressive: **will** + **be** + present participle	*will be playing*
Future Perfect: **will** + **have** + past participle	*will have played*
Future Perfect Progressive: **will** + **have** + **been** + present participle	*will have been playing*

For information about irregular verb forms see pages 101–2.

Present and Present Perfect

Simple Present and Present Progressive

We use the Simple Present for permanent situations (1) and things that are generally true (2).

1 *Giraffes* **live** *in Africa. They* **have** *very long legs and necks. They* **feed** *on acacia leaves.*
2 *It* **snows** *a lot in January.* • *Birds* **don't sing** *at night.* • **Do** *women* **live** *longer than men?*

We also use the Simple Present for habits (3), things that happen regularly (4), with verbs that describe current states (5), and in informal reports or instructions (6).

3 *I* **bite** *my nails.* • *She* **drinks** *tea.* • **Does** *he usually* **wear** *socks with sandals?*
4 *They* **play** *bingo on Monday nights.* • *Her parents* **go** *to Muskoka every summer.*
5 *She* **loves** *chocolate.* • *They* **don't believe** *us.* • *He* **owns** *his condo.* (NOT ~~He is owning his condo.~~)
6 *It* **says** *here the strike is over.* • *Bozak* **passes** *to Kessel, who* **shoots.** • *You* **go** *to the end and* **turn** *left.*

When we perform an action by speaking—for example when we promise to do something—we usually use the Simple Present, not the Present Progressive.

7 *I* **accept** *their decision.* • *I* **promise** *to be more careful.* (NOT ~~I'm promising to be more careful.~~)
Other verbs used like this include **admit, apologize, bet, deny, insist, regret**

We use the Present Progressive for actions in progress or to indicate being in the middle of an activity.

8 *Hi. I'm* **calling** *to let you know I'm* **coming,** *but it's* **snowing** *and the traffic* **is moving** *slowly.*

We can describe current situations as permanent with the Simple Present (9) or as temporary with the Present Progressive (10).

9 *My brother Kim* **lives** *in Vancouver and* **works** *for a magazine. He* **writes** *about economics.*
10 *My sister Fiona* **is living** *with Kim right now. She* **isn't working** *yet. She's* **looking** *for a job.*

We can use **be** and **have** in the Simple Present for a typical situation or state (11) and in the Present Progressive for a temporary or special situation (12).

11 *Wendy's normally a quiet person. She* **has** *a gentle voice.* (NOT ~~She's having a gentle voice.~~)
12 *Wendy's* **being** *wild tonight. She's* **having** *a party.* (NOT ~~She has a party.~~)

Present Perfect and Present Perfect Progressive

We use the Present Perfect to refer to or describe an action or situation started in the past that connects to the present (13), when we mean "at any point up to now" (14), and with stative verbs (15).

13 *How long* **have** *you* **worked** *here? ~ I've* **worked** *here since 2010.* (NOT ~~I work here since 2010.~~)
14 *This is the best coffee I* **have** *ever* **tasted.** • *I* **haven't been** *to an opera, but I've* **seen** *one on TV.*
15 *I* **have known** *Tony for about five years.* (NOT ~~I know him for five years. / I've been knowing him for five years.~~)

We use the Present Perfect Progressive when we refer to an activity in progress up to the present (16) and to ask about or describe actions that go on over a period of time up to the present (17).

16 *They've* **been paving** *our street and it's* **been causing** *a lot of traffic problems.*
17 **Have** *you* **been waiting** *long? ~ I've* **been sitting** *here for an hour.* (NOT ~~Are you waiting long?~~)

We use the Present Perfect Progressive to describe something as if it is a continuous action up to the present (18) and the Present Perfect to describe it as a series of separate actions (19).

18 *He's* **been calling** *for you.* • *It* **has been raining** *a lot recently.* (NOT ~~It's raining a lot recently.~~)
19 *He* **has called** *four times and he* **has asked** *for you each time.* (NOT ~~He has been calling four times.~~)

We can describe an action as a process going on from earlier up to the present (Present Perfect Progressive) (20) or as the present result of an earlier action (Present Perfect) (21).

20 *We've* **been making** *chicken soup. That's why the kitchen is hot and steamy.*
21 *We've* **made** *chicken soup. That's what everyone is eating. Would you like some?*

A Complete each paragraph with one set of verbs, using the Simple Present or Present Progressive.

know / look / not be / fix / use   be / be / have / say / tell   be / live / look / move / resemble

My computer (1) _is_ very frustrating right now. Every time I (2) _use_ it to save something, it (3) _says_ it (4) _has_ no space in its memory, which (5) _is_ ridiculous.

Whales and dolphins (6) _look_ like fish, but they (7) _are_ mammals that (8) _live_ in the ocean and (9) _move_ through water in ways that (10) _resembles_ the movements of a dog rather than those of a shark.

Man: Excuse me. I (11) _am looking_ for Ms. Fajardo, but she (12) _isn't_ in her usual classroom. (13) _Do_ you _know_ where she is?

Woman: Oh, they (14) _are fixing_ her classroom ceiling this week so she (15) _uses_ the library as her classroom.

B Using a dictionary if necessary, complete these sentences with the nouns and the verbs in the Present Perfect.

also-ran	hat trick
has-been	no-show

buy	not come	say	train
hear	not finish	take	win

1 Henrik _has won_ the race for the second year in a row and he _has said_ that he will come back and try to make it a _hat trick_ next year.

2 An "_also-ran_" is an informal term for a person or a horse that _has taken_ part in a competition or a race, but _has not come_ first, second, or third.

3 Jeff says he _has heared_ people describe him negatively as a "_has been_," but he _has trained_ hard this year to prove that he's still one of the best.

4 A "_no show_" is an informal expression for someone who _has bought_ a ticket for an event, a trip, etc., but who _has not come_ to the event.

C Choose an answer (a–d) for each question (1–4) and add these verbs in the Present Perfect or the Present Perfect Progressive.

be, complete, do, know, read, show, swim

1 How long _have been_ she and Mark _knowing_ each other? (_C_)

2 Why is your hair all wet? (_b_)

3 _Have_ you _completed_ an application form? (_d_)

4 _Have_ you _shown_ Keith the report yet? (_ _)

a Yes, he _has been reading_ it for the past hour.

b I _have_ just _swum_.

c They _have been_ friends since school.

d Yes, I _have_ already _done_ that.

D Correct the mistakes in this text.

My neighbour is named Jeanine. She ~~is coming~~ _comes_ from Belgium. She is living [_has been_] here since 2009 and she says she has been going [_gone_] back to visit her family in Belgium only once. She's having [_comes_] an accent that is the same as people who ~~are coming~~ _comes_ from France, but I never ask [_have asked_] her if she is speaking [_speaks_] French. She is really liking [_likes_] to go to the theatre and she is inviting [_has invited_] me to go with her one Saturday. In the short time I am knowing [_have been_] her, we become [_became_] good friends.

TENSES · PAGE 13

Past and Past Perfect

Simple Past and Past Progressive

We use the Simple Past for completed actions in the past (1) and past states (2).

  1 *Richler **wrote** Barney's Version.* • *Edison **invented** the lightbulb.* • *Anne Murray **sang** "Snowbird."*

  2 *Life **seemed** easier then.* • *That ring **belonged** to my mother.* (NOT *~~It was belonging to my mother.~~*)

We use the Simple Past for two or more past actions in sequence, especially in narrative.

  3 *I **tripped** and **landed** on my knees.* • *He **knocked** her down, **grabbed** her purse, and **ran** off.* •
    *He **took** off his hat and **came** forward. The floorboards **creaked** under his boots.*

To describe habits in the past or to make a stronger contrast with the present, we can use the form **used to** (4). The negative is **didn't use to** or (more formally) **used not to** (5). We can also use **would** to refer to typical actions or activities during a period in the past (6).

  4 *There **used to be** a store on the corner.* • *He **used to swim** a lot.* (NOT *~~He was used to swim a lot.~~*)

  5 ***Didn't** they **use to hang** people?* • *We **didn't use to have** a car.* • *They **used not to be** enemies.*

  6 *In summer, we **would take** trips to the beach.* • *We **would** sometimes **buy** fresh strawberries.*

We use the Past Progressive to describe actions in progress at a specific time in the past.

  7 *What **were** you **doing** at 8:30 last night?* ~ *I **wasn't doing** anything special. I **was** just reading.* •
    *During the 1990s, many people **were leaving** the East Coast and **moving** to the West to look for work.*

We can use the Past Progressive with some verbs (**wonder, hope**) to make a request more polite.

  8 *I **was wondering** when I could talk to you.* • *We **were hoping** you might have a free moment.*

We can use the Simple Past when we want to describe a past activity as a series of separate actions (9) and the Past Progressive to describe the past activity as if it was a continuous action (10). In many cases, the Simple Past and Past Progressive can be used interchangeably.

  9 *Usually she **went** to the library about once a week and only **studied** occasionally for tests.*

  10 *Before the final exam, however, she **was going** to the library and **studying** every single day.*

In sentences with **when**- and **while**-clauses, we can use the Past Progressive to describe an activity in one clause that starts before an action in another clause (11). The activity that starts later may interrupt the first activity (12).

  11 *While he **was driving**, I **fell** asleep.* • *We **saw** Erdem while we **were walking** in the park.*

  12 *I **was listening** to the news when she **phoned**.* • *When I **was running**, I **slipped** and **fell**.*

Note the difference between *When she came back, we were watching TV* (= We were watching before she came back) and *When she came back, we watched TV* (= We watched after she came back).

Past Perfect and Past Perfect Progressive

We use the Past Perfect when we are describing an action with the Simple Past and we want to refer to an action further in the past (13). We also use the Past Perfect for earlier events after clauses with reporting or thinking verbs in the past (14).

  13 *We went to his office, but he **had left**.* • *Susan didn't have the money because she **had spent** it.*

  14 *Nikhil told me our team **had scored** twice.* • *I thought we **had won**.* (NOT *~~I thought we have won.~~*)

We use the Past Perfect Progressive for events in progress before another event in the past.

  15 *I **had been thinking** about that before you mentioned it.*

Stative verbs are not used in this way. (NOT *~~I had been knowing about that before you mentioned it.~~*)

We can describe an action as a process going on before a past event (Past Perfect Progressive) (16). We can also describe it as the result of an action before a past event (Past Perfect) (17).

  16 *We **had been making** chicken soup so the kitchen was still hot and steamy when she came in.*

  17 *We **had made** chicken soup and so we offered her some when she came in.*

A Complete each paragraph with one set of verbs, using the Simple Past or Past Progressive.

miss / not get / wonder   break / see / steal / teach
come / listen / make / say   explain / talk / understand

We (1) _were listening_ to music when one of the neighbours (2) _came_ to the door and (3) _said_ she couldn't sleep because we (4) _were making_ too much noise.

Someone (5) _broke_ into Nala's office and (6) _stole_ her computer yesterday afternoon while she (7) _was teaching_ her history class. No one (8) _saw_ the thief.

Because he never (9) _explained_ anything very clearly, none of us (10) _understood_ what the science teacher (11) _was talking_ about most of the time.

I'm sorry. I (12) _didn't come_ here on time and I (13) _missed_ the beginning of your presentation, but I (14) _was wondering_ if you might have an extra handout left.

B Complete the text with these verbs in the **Past Perfect** or **Past Perfect Progressive**.

be, catch, live, plan, take, break, have, make, remove, worry

The telephone call from the police was a shock, but not a complete surprise. Tanya (1) _had been worried_ constantly about the old house lying empty during the two months since her mother went into the hospital. She (2) _had planned_ to stop by and check the empty place, but she (3) _had been_ extra busy at work recently. According to the police, a man (4) _had broken_ into the house. They (5) _caught_ him one morning as he was leaving the building with one of her mother's large paintings. When Tanya walked into the house, it was obvious that the man (6) _had been living_ there for quite a while. He (7) _had been taking_ food from the cupboards and throwing empty cans and packages all over the floor. He (8) _had made_ quite a mess. He (9) _had_ also _removed_ several paintings from the walls. Tanya decided not to tell her mother because she (10) _was_ _been having_ already enough pain in recent weeks and really didn't need any more bad news.

C Correct the mistakes in the use of tenses in this text.

A few years ago, when my friend and I were ~~drive~~ _driving_ across the Prairies, we sometimes ~~stop~~ _stopped_ for the night in a park or a field. If it wasn't ~~rain~~ _raining_, we just ~~sleep~~ _slept_ outside in our sleeping bags under the stars. We really ~~enjoying~~ _enjoyed_ that. If it was ~~rain~~ _raining_, we put up our small tent and ~~crawl~~ _crawled_ inside for the night. One night, while we ~~sleep~~ _were sleeping_ in the tent, I think that the ground ~~moving~~ _was moving_ under me. I ~~sit~~ _sat_ up and I ~~realize~~ _realized_ that the tent was ~~try~~ _trying_ to move and only the weight of our bodies was ~~hold~~ _holding_ it in place. When we ~~get~~ _got_ outside, we ~~discover~~ _discovered_ that we ~~stand~~ _were standing_ ankle-deep in a small stream and our tent slowly ~~floats~~ _was floating_ away. At first, we really _were_ surprised and worried, but then we ~~think~~ _thought_ it ~~is~~ _was_ very funny.

Modals

The modals are a group of auxiliary verbs (**can, could, may, might, must, ought, shall, should, will, would**) that we can use with other verbs to say what is possible, permitted, necessary, and so on.

The phrasal modals are a group of verb phrases (**be able to, be allowed to, be going to, be supposed to, have to, need to**) that can be used instead of modals.

A **Read through this text and find**

Should never *won't increase you luck*

1 another negative modal

They will be able to

2 a sentence that contains three different modals

A Superstitions are beliefs that some things can't be explained by reason and that there are certain objects or actions that bring good or bad luck. Most superstitions are old and
5 people usually have no idea where they came from. We may be told, for example, that we should never open an umbrella indoors because that will bring bad luck. We aren't told why or what kind of bad thing might happen to
10 us, but few of us are going to try to find out.

B Everyone knows that thirteen is an unlucky number. Other things that can bring bad luck include breaking a mirror, walking under a ladder, or spilling salt. At least when
15 you spill salt, you can avoid the bad luck by immediately throwing some of the salt over your left shoulder with your right hand. Unfortunately, the man sitting behind you at that moment will suddenly get a shower of salt
20 all over him. Obviously, he must have done something earlier that brought him bad luck.

C If you ask people why it is bad luck to walk under a ladder, they usually say that it's because something might fall on your head
25 It could be a hammer, a brick, a piece of wood, paint, or water. It is interesting that the superstition is explained in terms of such ordinary things. The origin of the superstition is much darker and more scary. According to
30 the *Oxford Guide to British and American Culture*, "this idea may have developed out of the practice in medieval times of hanging criminals from ladders."

D More confusing are those superstitions
35 that seem to have different meanings for different people. Some people will tell you that it is bad luck if a black cat walks in front of you. Others will say that seeing a black cat is supposed to be lucky. Other tokens of good
40 luck are a rabbit's foot (not lucky for the rabbit, obviously), a special coin, a four-leaf clover, and a horseshoe. If you hang the horseshoe over your front door to bring luck to your house, you must be careful to have the open end pointing
45 upwards. If you hang it the other way, your good luck will just drop out through the gap. You can also wish for good luck by crossing your fingers. You don't have to cross all of them, only the middle finger over the index finger.

50 **E** There are special phrases that people use to bring luck. There's "Good luck," of course. Another expression is "Touch wood" or "Knock on wood." This is usually heard when people talk about their good luck or when they are
55 hoping that they will be able to get or do something they want. By using the expression, the speaker tries to avoid having any bad luck that might be caused by talking about having good luck. If there isn't anything wooden to
60 touch, some people will tap themselves on the head as they say "Touch wood." However, acting as if you have a wooden head, touching it with your fingers crossed and saying "Knock on wood" all at once won't necessarily
65 increase your luck.

B **Choose one of the following as the final sentence of each of the paragraphs A–E above.**

1 People will just think you're very superstitious or possibly crazy. (E)
2 That explanation makes the superstition much easier to understand. (C)
3 With your fingers like this, however, it may be hard to nail that horseshoe over your door. (D)
4 We just don't open one until we are outside. (A)
5 Perhaps he had opened an umbrella indoors. (B)

Modals are single words that always have the same form.
  1 We **should** wait for Enrique. He **may** come soon. (NOT ~~He mays come soon.~~)
Other modals include **can**, **could**, **might**, **must**, **ought**, **shall**, **will**, **would**

We use modals before the base forms of other verbs.
  2 I **can wait** for him. • You **must leave**. (NOT ~~I can waiting for him. You must to leave.~~)
Ought is always followed by **to**: You **ought to** go home. (NOT ~~You ought go home.~~)

We do not use **do** with modals in questions (3) or negatives (4).
  3 **Will** it work? • **Can** you play the piano? (NOT ~~Do you can play the piano?~~)
  4 She **might not** want it. • I **couldn't** swim very fast. (NOT ~~I didn't could swim very fast.~~)

The modals **shall**, **will**, and **would** are usually contracted (5), unless they are being emphasized (6).
  5 **I'll** bring you one, okay? • He**'ll** be there, **won't** he? • She**'d** like to stay, wouldn't she?
  6 Do not forget! We **will** leave at 8 a.m. precisely. We **will not** wait for latecomers.

We usually use the forms **could**, **might**, and **would** in clauses after past tense verbs (7), especially in indirect speech (8).
  7 I didn't know she **could** speak Spanish. • I was hoping you **might** give me some advice.
  8 ("Can I help?") She asked if she **could** help. • ("I'll be late.") He said he **would** be late.

We don't put two modals together before a verb. See (11) below.
  9 We **can win** this game and we **will win** it! (NOT ~~We will can win this game!~~)

Phrasal modals

Phrasal modals are verb phrases beginning with **be** or **have** that can be used instead of modals.
  10 Most 18-year-olds **are able to** take care of themselves. (= They **can** take care of themselves.)
      However, we **have to** make sure that they have support. (= We **must** OR We **should** make sure …)
Other examples are **be allowed to** (can / may), **be going to** (will), **be supposed to** (should), **need to** (must)

We always use phrasal modals instead of modals in five structures: after a modal (11), where an infinitive (12) or a gerund (13) is needed, and in the perfect (14) and progressive (15) forms.
  11 We **will be able to** win this game! • They **may be going to** increase tuition next year.
  12 He seems **to be able to** do everything • I hope **to be allowed to** stay.
  13 I love **being able to** sit outside in the sun. • I hate **having to** repeat everything.
  14 They **have had to** wait for hours. • They **haven't been allowed to** leave the building.
  15 She **is having to** pay extra. • We **aren't being allowed to** take the test early.
We can use two phrasal modals together: I**'m going to have to** go to the store for more bread.

C **Find the three sentences in the text on page 16 that contain both a modal and a phrasal modal.**

Few of us are going to try to find out
He must have done something brought bad
They will be able to get or do something
they want.

Ability and permission

Ability: can, could, be able to

We use **can** when we refer to general ability and **could** for general ability in the past.
   1 *Can you play chess?* • *Ostriches can run very fast.* • *Their son could swim before he could walk.*
In the negative, **can't** is more common than **cannot** (written as one word), which is formal.
(NOT ~~I can not go.~~)

We often use **can** and **could** with verbs for mental processes (2) and senses (3).
   2 *I couldn't decide.* • *Can you remember her name?* (NOT ~~Are you remembering her name?~~)
   3 *We could hear a cat, but we couldn't see it.* • *I can smell onions.* (NOT ~~I'm smelling onions.~~)
We sometimes use these verbs in the Simple Present (*I smell onions*), but not in the Present Progressive.
Other verbs used like this include **believe, feel, guess, taste, understand**

We use **be able to** (not **can** or **could**) in four of the phrasal modal structures: in infinitives,
in gerunds (4), after modals, and in the perfect (5).
   4 *They want to be able to practise.* • *She left without being able to talk to the teacher.*
   5 *I won't be able to finish.* • *He hasn't been able to study.* (NOT ~~He hasn't could study.~~)
We don't use **be able to** in the progressive: *He isn't able to walk.* (NOT ~~He isn't being able to walk.~~)

We sometimes use **am/is/are able to** instead of **can** for general ability in formal situations (6).
We use **was/were able to** (not **could**) for the achievement of something difficult in the past (7).
   6 *Is the child able to tie her shoelaces without help?*
   7 *We had a flat tire, but we were able to fix it and keep driving.* (NOT *... ~~but we could fix it.~~*)
We can use **couldn't** to say something difficult was not achieved: *We couldn't fix it.*

We use **could** (not **can** or **be able to**) plus the perfect to refer to an ability or opportunity not used.
   8 *He could have done very well, but he was lazy.* (NOT ~~He can have done very well.~~)
Note the difference between **I was able to win** (= I won) and **I could have won** (= I didn't win).

A Using a dictionary if necessary, complete each sentence with one pair of words, plus appropriate forms of *can, could,* or *be able to.*

difficult / managed	fly / swimming	stay / unflappable
feel / numb	illiterate / read	successful / tried

1 Penguins are birds that ...*can't fly*..., but ...*are able to*...
   use their wings for ...*swimming*... .
2 An ...*unflappable*... person is someone who ...*can stay*...
   calm in difficult situations.
3 It was so cold that my fingers were ...*numb*... and I ...*couldn't feel*... anything.
4 When people are ...*illiterate*..., they ...*can't read*... or write.
5 A ...*successful*... person is someone who has ...*been able*...
   do what he or she ...*tried*... to do.
6 If you ...*managed*... to finish a task, it means you ...*could*...
   do it, even though it was ...*difficult*... .

B Complete this joke with appropriate forms of *can* or *could.*

Did you hear about the woman who went fishing, but (1) ...*couldn't*... catch anything? On her
way home, she stopped at the market so that she (2) ...*could*... buy two fish. She then
stepped back a few paces and asked the fish seller if he (3) ...*could*... throw them to her.
The puzzled man asked, "Why?" The woman answered, "So that I (4) ...*can*... tell my
husband that I caught a couple of fish today!"

Permission: **can, could, may, might, be allowed to**

We use **can** and **could** to ask for permission, choosing **could** to be more polite (9). We use **can** (not **could**) to give or refuse permission (10).

> 9 **Can** *I borrow your dictionary?* • **Can** *the dog come into the house?* • **Could** *we leave early today?*
>
> 10 *Yes, you* **can**. • *No, it* **can't**. • *I'm sorry, but you* **can't**. (NOT ~~I'm sorry, but you couldn't.~~)

In formal situations, we can use **may** when we ask for (11) or give (12) permission (or not).

> 11 **May** *we come in?* • **May** *I take this chair?* • **May** *I use one of these phones?*
>
> 12 *Yes, you* **may**. • *No, you* **may not**, *because I need it.* • *Of course, you* **may** *use any of these phones.*

Might can be used to ask for, but not to give, permission: **Might** *we be able to go inside? ~ Yes.* (NOT ~~Yes, you might.~~)

We usually use **can** (not **may**) when we describe laws and rules (13). **May** (not **might**) is sometimes used in formal rules (14).

> 13 *You* **can't** *park here. ~ Why not? ~ I think only buses and taxis* **can** *park here.*
>
> 14 *No food or drinks* **may** *be brought inside.* • *Pedestrians* **may not** *cross here.*

We use **be allowed to** (not **may** or **might**) when we emphasize getting permission on a specific occasion (15) and in all the phrasal modal structures (16).

> 15 *That day was the first time I* **was allowed to** *make my own breakfast.* (NOT ~~I might make~~ ...)
>
> 16 *No one* **has been allowed to** *see the test results.* • *We* **aren't being allowed to** *go in yet.*

Note the combination *You* **may/might be allowed to** *go.* (= It's possible you'll get permission to go.)

C **Choose an ending (a–f) for each beginning (1–6) and add *can, may,* or *be allowed to*.**

1 New students ...Can........... not register (C) a as if he were interested in my drawing.
2 Children shouldn't .be allowed to.(d) b because there's no more work to do.
3 He casually asked, "...Can....... I see that?" (a.) c for more than three classes.
4 You might not .be allowed to. go in (e.) d eat or drink during a test.
5 You ...may......... all leave early today (b) e if you're under 19.
6 They are unlikely to .be allowed to.(f.) f play with matches.

D **Correct the mistakes in this text.**

My friend Dana <s>can not</s> *(can't)* say "No." If another student asks her, "Can I borrow your pen?", she always

says, "Of course, you could *(can)*," and hands it over, even when she only has one pen and it means she isn't

being able to do her own work. After I heard her do that one day, I told her that she can have said, *(could have)*

"Sorry, but you cannot, *(not)* because I only have one pen." In reply, she said, "But how do they could do *(can)*

their work without a pen?" I knew that I can *(could)* have tried to answer that question, but somehow I

didn't think I'll can change how she behaved, no matter what I said.
(Could)

Possibility

Possibility: **may** and **might**

We can use either **may** or **might** to say that something is possible now or later (1). We use either **may** or **might** plus the perfect to say it is possible that something happened before now (2).

   1 *Taking these pills **may/might** cause drowsiness. You **might/may** fall asleep at the wheel.*
   2 *I **may/might have lost** my key.* • *Tanya **might/may have met** Saj when she was in Montreal.*
In the negative, we can say *It may not/might not happen.* (NOT ~~It mayn't happen.~~)

We use **may** (not **might**) when we say that a possible situation is common or usual (3). We can use **might** (not **may**) in descriptions of what was possible in the past (4) and when we report speech and thoughts after verbs in the past tense (5).

   3 *Peppers **may** be green, yellow, or red.* • *Measles **may** cause a fever and small red spots.*
   4 *In those days, people **might** spend their entire lives in the village where they were born.*
   5 *("I may be late.") He said he **might** be late.* • *I was wondering if you **might** have time to read this.*

Possibility: **can** and **could**

We use **can/could** in general statements to say that a situation is (**can**) or was (**could**) possible.

   6 *Some dogs **can** be very dangerous.* • *The old house **could** be quite cold, even in summer.*

We use **could** (not **can**) when we speculate about things, meaning "It's possible that …" (7) and to ask "Is it possible that …?" (8).

   7 *Your purse **could** be in the car.* • *It **could** rain this weekend.* (NOT ~~It can rain this weekend.~~)
   8 *Peter is late. **Could** he be stuck in traffic?* (NOT ~~Can he be stuck in traffic?~~)

We use **could** (not **can**) plus the perfect when we speculate about the possibility of an earlier event.

   9 *The bank **could have closed** already.* • *You **could have fallen**.* (NOT ~~You can have fallen.~~)

May/might or can/could?

We use **may**, **might**, or **could** (not **can**) to say that a specific event is possible (10), before phrasal modals (11), and before the progressive or perfect (12). We can use **might** or **could** plus the perfect to express irritation at someone's not having done something (13).

   10 *Ava **may** arrive later.* • *There **could** be a storm tonight.* (NOT ~~There can be a storm tonight.~~)
   11 *It **may** be going to rain.* • *We **might** have to leave soon.* (NOT ~~We can have to leave soon.~~)
   12 *The economy **may be showing** signs of recovery.* • *Lani **might have borrowed** the hair dryer.*
   13 *You **might have gotten** me a coffee when you went out to get yours!*

We use **may** or **might** (not **can** or **could**) when we make a concession before a clause with **but**.

   14 *She **may** be seventy, **but** she still likes to dance.* • *We **might** have lost a battle, **but** not the war.*
Note that *It may be old, but it works* is very similar in meaning to *Although it's old, it works.*

We use **can** or **could** (not **may** or **might**) to make suggestions about possible actions (15) and when we ask people to do things (16).

   15 *We have a simple choice. We **can/could** wait here for a bus or we **could/can** start walking.*
   16 ***Can** you show me where it is?* • ***Could** you take this away?* (NOT ~~May you take this away?~~)

We use **may not** or **might not** when we mean "possibly not" (17). When we mean "not possible," we use **can't** for the present situation and **couldn't** for the past (18).

   17 *It **may/might not** be true.* (= Perhaps not) • *This bill **may/might not** be right. It seems too high.*
   18 *That story **can't** be true.* (= I'm sure it's not) • *This bill **can't** be right. We only had two coffees.* •
     *I knew the rumour about your accident **couldn't** be true because I'd seen you that morning.*

A Using a dictionary if necessary, complete each sentence with an adjective and a modal.

absurd, feasible, theoretical, may, may be, might, disqualified, potential, undecided, may not (×2), may have, might not

1 Your uncle ...may have... run in a marathon when he was younger, but it's ...absurd... to keep describing him as "one of the top runners."

2 She ...may be... breaking the rules and will possibly be ...disqualified... from the rest of the competition.

3 If someone is ...undecided... about an action, they ...may... or ...may not... do it.

4 We knew about the ...potential... problems and the workmen had said they ...might not... finish on time.

5 Your plan ...may not... be approved because people don't think it's economically ...feasible...

6 From a ...theoretical... perspective, that ...might... happen, but nobody thinks it will.

B Complete the text with appropriate forms of *can* or *could* plus these verbs.

avoid, be, not imagine, pick, save, not send

These days, when we (1) ...can pick... up a phone and call anywhere in the world, we really don't realize, and often (2) ...can't imagin... , how difficult long-distance communication (3) ...could be... for people in the past. In the early nineteenth century the Treaty of Ghent brought an end to the War of 1812 between Britain and the United States. But the news (4) ...could n't sent... across the Atlantic fast enough to stop General Andrew Jackson from attacking and defeating the British forces in New Orleans a full three weeks after the treaty was signed. With better communication, the battle (5) ...could be avoided... and the lives of more than two thousand people (6) ...could be saved...

C Correct the mistakes in these sentences using *may*, *might*, *can*, or *could*.

► It was a bad accident. We ~~can~~ **could** have been killed.

1 They ~~can~~ **might** be going to increase airport fees to pay for increased security.

2 Don't turn off the computer yet. Someone ~~can~~ **may** still be using it.

3 In late eighteenth century Scotland, you ~~may~~ **might** be hanged for stealing a sheep.

4 These people ~~can~~ **may** have a lot of money, but it doesn't make them interesting.

5 By Friday I ~~can~~ **may** have finished the book, but if I get too busy, I ~~can~~ **may** not.

6 ~~May~~ **Can** someone tell me where the main office is?

7 We know he doesn't tell the truth, so we really ~~might~~ **can** not believe any of his stories.

8 He asked me last night if you ~~may~~ **might** be willing to talk to Julita for him.

9 According to the forecast, the weather ~~can~~ **may** be a bit warmer today.

10 This button isn't working. ~~May~~ **Could** the children have broken it?

Necessity

Necessity: **must** and **must not**

We use **must** to say that something is necessary (1), especially in orders and rules (2). We use the negative **must not** to tell people not to do things or to say something is a bad idea (3).

   1 Plants **must** have light. • Your basic needs are the things you **must** have to live a normal life.
   2 You **must** come to class on time. • Bike helmets **must** be worn. • All visitors **must** sign in.
   3 You **must not** come late. • Empty boxes **must not** be stacked in front of the emergency exit.

We also use **must** to encourage someone to do something we think is important (4) or to emphasize a strong feeling or opinion (5).

   4 We **must** have a party on Victoria Day. • You and I **must** get together for lunch soon.
   5 I **must** disagree with that. We **must not** accept new regulations that restrict our civil rights.

Necessity: **have to**, **don't have to**, and **have got to**

We usually use **have to** instead of **must** when we are not in control of what is necessary or required.

   6 My mother **has to** have an operation on her knee. • I **have to** wear glasses for reading.

We usually use **have to** (with auxiliary **do**) instead of **must** in questions.

   7 Why **does** everyone **have to** sign in? • **Don't** you **have to** wear a seat belt? • **Do** I **have to** do it again?
We can form questions with **must**, but they sound more formal: Must I do it again?

We use **have to** (not **must**) when we ask about or refer to what was required or necessary in the past (8) and in all the phrasal modal structures (9).

   8 **Did** you **have to** wear a uniform in school? Alessandro **had to** wear a jacket and tie.
   9 You **will have to** change. • I don't want to **have to** fight. • Nobody likes **having to** wash dishes. •
      I **have had to** complete three forms already. Now I'**m having to** complete another one.

We use **don't have to** (not **must not**) as the opposite of **must** when something is not necessary.

   10 It's free—you **don't have to** pay. • The door was open so we **didn't have to** wait outside.

We can use **don't have to** instead of **have to** in informal situations, but only in the present tense (11).
We use **have** (not **do**) as an auxiliary with **got to** when we form negatives and questions (12).

   11 We **have got to** find a better way to do this. • I'**ve got to** see Ben. (NOT I had got to see Ben.)
   12 She **hasn't got to** wait long. • **Have** we **got to** buy tickets? (NOT Do we have got to buy tickets?)

Necessity: **need to**, **don't need to**, and **didn't need to**

We can use **need to** like **have to** to say that something is necessary (13) or not necessary (14).

   13 Ramy **needs to** / **has to** leave soon. • I'll **need to**/**have to** take an umbrella. (NOT I'll need take an
      umbrella.)
   14 We **don't need to**/**have to** wait. • Because it rained, I **won't need to**/**have to** water the garden.

We use **didn't need to** when we mean it was not necessary to do something (15) or when we mean something unnecessary was done (16).

   15 I knew there wouldn't be a test, so I **didn't need to** study. I watched TV instead.
   16 I studied all night, then found out the test was cancelled. I **didn't need to** study at all.

A Using a dictionary if necessary, complete the sentences with these words and appropriate forms of *must* or *have to*.

command, duty-free, evil, extra, fruit, obligation, step, taboo

1 An optional .... in a new car is something that is available, but you .... get it.
2 An essential .... is a part of a procedure you'll .... do in order for it to be successful.
3 Forbidden .... is something that you .... touch or have, even though you really want it.
4 In the army, soldiers .... always obey a .... given by a senior officer.
5 If you are under no .... to do something, you .... do it.
6 When you buy things that are ...., you .... pay tax on them.
7 If a topic is .... in a particular culture, it means that you .... talk about it because it is considered offensive.
8 A necessary .... is something you don't like or want, but which you may .... accept in order to achieve your goal.

B Complete the sentences with these verbs and adjectives.

didn't have to, must, need to, allowed, official, significant, having to, must not, didn't need to, impossible, required, unnecessary

1 I .... wear a jacket and tie last night. Formal attire was not ....
2 You .... make so much noise. All that shouting was ....
3 People .... have dogs in their rooms. Pets are not .... in the hotel.
4 You won't .... fill out any forms. All the .... paperwork will be complete.
5 Not .... pay to use the pool is a .... benefit of being a student here.
6 Everyone .... have a valid passport because it will be .... to enter the country without one.

C Correct the mistakes in these sentences.

1 We have already washed all the dinner dishes so you must not clean them tonight.

2 Everyone will have got to go through metal detectors every time they enter the building.

3 I'll need get some medicine because I've got a terrible headache and I have to keep working.

4 The part that broke is a crucial component and I must to find a replacement immediately.

5 Whenever gratuity is included in a bill, customers don't need leave a tip for the waiter.

6 Our train arrived late and so we had got to take a taxi to get to our meeting on time.

7 I don't want to be the one to must have to tell him that he failed the entrance exam again.

8 I'm sure you don't need be over eighteen to go into a bar here, but we must ask someone.

9 When we stayed with my grandmother, we must go to the store with her every Saturday.

10 We didn't know that our friends had already gone into the theatre so we didn't need wait all that time for them outside in the cold.

The passive

Passive verbs, or passives, are formed with **be** plus the past participle of a transitive verb (*My car **was stolen***). We use passive verbs to say what happens to the subject (*Two men **were arrested***) in contrast to active verbs that are used to say what the subject does (*The police **arrested** two men*).

A Read through this text and find two more examples of the same verb (*find* and *move*) being used as both an active and a passive verb.

For as long as people can remember, small towns like Stone Creek and Pineville in northern Alabama have been hit by storms every spring. They are as predictable as the apple
5 blossoms that are always shaken loose from the trees and blown along the country roads. Some trees may be knocked over or the roof of a building might be slightly damaged, but usually the effects of the storms are more inconvenient than deadly. This year
10 was different.

Last night, a powerful storm roared into the area, sending devastating tornadoes spinning through the small farming communities. It destroyed farms, schools, and churches and buried people in
15 the ruins of their own homes. It transformed the landscape. Herds of cattle that had been moved into barns for safety are nowhere to be seen, nor are the barns. Other buildings where tractors and equipment were being stored seem to have been
20 completely blown away.

The scenes of devastation this morning are described by one rescue worker as "like the end of the world." Since first light, rescue crews have been moving through the countryside, looking for
25 survivors. Small teams have had to be flown in to some areas by helicopter because the roads have been blocked by dozens of fallen trees. In other areas, rescuers don't know what they will find as

they search through the debris. "We're guessing that
30 there are some people who may have been pinned down under their own ceilings," says Greg Hayden, a firefighter from Atlanta. "Sometimes we can't tell the houses from the stables or the garages. It's a mess. Dozens of people and animals could have
35 been buried in there."

One by one, the miracles and the tragedies are coming to light. Jim Clinton, having been warned of the approaching storm on his radio, drove his wife and daughter to his local church. He thought it
40 would be safer there than staying in his small house. Two of the church walls collapsed, but after being trapped inside for four hours, the Clintons were found alive by rescuers this morning. Not far away, an old couple had retreated to the basement of their
45 home as the storm approached. Tragically, they were both killed when part of a wall crashed through the floor on top of them. The names of all victims are being withheld until their families can be notified.

At least 38 people have died and many more are
50 missing. About 100 people have been seriously injured and more than 1000 have been left homeless. The search for the missing may last for days, but the effects of this one storm are going to be felt for many years. "It's like someone dropped a bomb,"
55 said one shocked woman as she searched through the remains of what used to be her home. ●

B Complete this summary using appropriate forms of <u>verbs</u> from the text.

At least 38 people have died, about 100 (1) .. have been .... seriously
injured ...., and more than 1000 (2) .. have been left ...... homeless
in northern Alabama after the area (3) ... have been hit ..... by a powerful storm last
night. Farms, schools, and churches (4) ... were destroyed .... and some people
(5) were buried .... in the ruins of their own homes. Fallen trees
(6) .... blocked .... roads in some areas, so rescue teams
(7) .. had to by flown .. by helicopter. The effects of this storm
(8) .. would last .... for years.

Active and passive

We use an active verb to say what the subject does (1) and a passive verb to say what happens to the subject (2).

1 *After the accident, someone **called** the police and they **arrested** the drunk driver.*
2 *After the accident, the police **were called** and the drunk driver **was arrested**.*

We use the object of an active verb as the subject of a passive verb (3). We can't create passives from intransitive verbs (4).

3 *We clear **the table** and wash **the dishes**. → **The table** is cleared and **the dishes** are washed.*
4 *We swam every day. • Garrick came later.* (NOT ~~Garrick was come later.~~)

A passive verb has two parts. We use a form of the verb **be** plus a past participle.

5 *You have to rewrite the first paragraph. → The first paragraph has to **be rewritten**.*

We can use a **by**-phrase after a passive verb to say who or what causes the action.

6 *My car was repaired **by Rosie**. • Some roads are blocked **by fallen trees**.*

C Passive tenses: Complete this table with one example of each type of passive from the text on page 24.

Simple Present passive: am / is / are + past participle
ACTIVE: *You place an order one day and they deliver your groceries the next.*
PASSIVE: *An order **is placed** one day and your groceries **are delivered** the next.*
1 An order has been placed one day and your groceries have been [*handwritten*]

Present Progressive passive: am / is / are + being + past participle
ACTIVE: *They are building a new school and creating two new roads for access.*
PASSIVE: *A new school **is being built** and two new roads **are being created** for access.*
2 ....

Present Perfect passive: have / has + been + past participle
ACTIVE: *I've prepared the turkey and peeled the potatoes.*
PASSIVE: *The turkey **has been prepared** and the potatoes **have been peeled**.*
3 ....

Simple Past passive: was / were + past participle
ACTIVE: *The airline cancelled our flight and stranded us in Vancouver.*
PASSIVE: *Our flight **was cancelled** and we **were stranded** in Vancouver.*
4 ....

Past Progressive passive: was / were + being + past participle
ACTIVE: *They were cleaning the floor and washing the windows earlier today.*
PASSIVE: *The floor **was being cleaned** and the windows **were being washed** earlier today.*
5 ....

Past Perfect passive: had + been + past participle
ACTIVE: *Everyone had warned me about the weather before I went to St. John's.*
PASSIVE: *I **had been warned** about the weather before I went to St. John's.*
6 ....

Passive verbs

Verbs with and without objects

We create passives from verbs that can have objects (transitive verbs) (1), not from verbs that don't have objects (intransitive verbs) (2).

1 *He repaired the bike. Then he painted it.* → *The bike **was repaired**. Then it **was painted**.*
2 *Nothing happened.* • *We arrived early.* (NOT *~~We were arrived early.~~*)

We usually create passives from verbs that describe actions (3), not states (4).

3 *They scored a goal in the last five minutes.* → *A goal **was scored** in the last five minutes.*
4 *My sister has two sons.* • *That belongs to me.* (NOT *~~That is belonged to me.~~*)

There are a few verbs that we usually use in the passive.

5 *Her parents **were married** in 1993 and she **was born** two years later.*

We create passives from transitive phrasal verbs (6), not from intransitive phrasal verbs (7).

6 *She locked her car. They broke into it.* → *Her car **was locked**. It **was broken into**.*
7 *Friends came over later.* • *My cold went away.* (NOT *~~My cold was gone away.~~*)

Verbs with two objects

We can create two passive structures when we use those verbs that can have an indirect object (**Maria**) and a direct object (**first prize**).

8 *They awarded Maria first prize.* → ***Maria was awarded** first prize.*
9 *They awarded first prize to Maria.* → ***First prize was awarded** to Maria.*
Other verbs like this include **give, hand, lend, pass, sell, send, show, teach, throw, write**

The passive structure we choose depends on which person or thing we want to refer to.

10 *No one taught us English.* → *English **wasn't taught** there.* OR *We **weren't taught** English.*

In the passive, we put the indirect object as subject or after the preposition **to**, not after the verb.

11 *He handed Cecilia a note.* → ***Cecilia** was handed a note.* OR *A note was handed **to Cecilia**.*
   (NOT *~~A note was handed Cecilia.~~*)

When a verb with two objects is used in only one active structure, we can only create one passive. If we can put the indirect object after the active verb, we can use it as subject of the passive.

12 *The judge fined him $250.* (NOT *~~The judge fined $250 to him.~~*) → *He **was fined** $250.*
   (NOT *~~$250 was fined to him.~~*)

If we can't put the indirect object after the active verb, we can't use it as subject of the passive.

13 *Then we explained our solutions to him.* → *Then our solutions **were explained** to him.*
   (NOT *~~We explained him our solutions.~~*) (NOT *~~He was explained our solutions.~~*)
Other verbs used like this include **demonstrate, describe, mention, present, report, suggest**

We can use a direct object as the subject of a passive, but not another noun that classifies it.

14 *Many people considered John Nash a genius.* → *John Nash **was considered** a genius.*
15 *They elected Joan mayor twice.* → *Joan **was elected** mayor twice.*
   (NOT *~~Mayor was elected Joan twice.~~*)

A **Rewrite each sentence with the verbs in the passive, where possible.**

1 Someone saw Narmatha outside the theatre as she was waiting to go in. She had a new hairstyle.

....

2 Karen feels sad because they didn't promote her and she has to pretend as if nothing happened.

....

3 She passes the puck to Palmeri. Palmeri tries to get past Jennings, but Jennings stops her.

....

B **Using a dictionary if necessary, choose an adjective for each blank and choose a, b, or both as correct sentences.**

illegible, inaudible, knowledgeable, reusable, impossible, inexplicable, ~~returnable~~, unspeakable

▶ It says here that your deposit isn't ... returnable ... .
   a It won't be given back. ✓   b You won't be given back. ...

1 He doesn't think it's .... to teach new tricks to old dogs.
   a He thinks they can be taught new tricks. ...   b He thinks tricks can be taught them. ...

2 His sudden disappearance remains .... We have no idea what happened.
   a We can't be explained. ...   b It can't be explained. ...

3 They think Raj Parvati is more .... about orchids than anyone else.
   a An expert is considered Raj Parvati. ...   b Raj Parvati is considered an expert. ...

4 She couldn't read us the note because of his .... handwriting.
   a We couldn't be read. ...   b It couldn't be read. ...

5 His first two or three sentences were ...., but he soon got more confident.
   a He spoke up. ...   b He was spoken up. ...

6 None of us will ever understand the .... suffering of the refugees.
   a We can never be described. ...   b It can never be described. ...

7 You can have one of these .... envelopes to send Marta the magazine.
   a Marta can be sent the magazine. ...   b The magazine can be sent to Marta. ...

C **Correct the mistakes in this text.**

The Christmas I remember best from my childhood ~~was~~ happened when I was about five, just after my younger sister born. Lots of people were come to our house with presents for us. I gave the job of taking the gifts and saying "Thank you." As each guest was arrived, I handed boxes or bags which filled with things that wrapped in Christmas paper. I told which ones were for me and which ones had to be place in a pile for my new sister. So many presents brought for us. I will never forget the experience of given so much. It really was a very special Christmas.

The uses of the passive

A Write the numbers of the appropriate examples in the spaces on this and the next page.

Focusing on what is done and who is affected

We use passives when we describe a process by referring to what is done, not who does it ____ , and when we report events, but we don't know, or it's not important, who performed the actions ____ .

1 *Wine **is made** from grapes.* • *Oranges **are grown** in Florida.* • *Bananas **have to be imported.***
2 *My purse **was stolen**.* • *Some trees **have been cut** down.* • *I think the old road **has been fixed**.*

We use passives to refer to the subject as the person or thing affected by the action ____ , often when that subject is the topic of two or more sentences ____ . We can use passives for several actions that affect the same subject in a single sentence ____ .

3 *Two people **were approached** in the park.* • *A tourist **was robbed**.* • *I **wasn't** badly **injured**.*
4 *After registration, courses **cannot be added**, **dropped**, or **changed** without permission.*
5 *The house is still for sale. It **was built** in 1928. It **was** completely **renovated** in 2010.*
The same subject can be used with different tenses: *It **was built** in 1928 and **is being renovated**.*

In informal situations, we use indefinite pronouns such as **someone** and generic pronouns such as **they** or **you** plus active verbs more than passives.

6 ***Someone** stole my purse.* • ***They** make wine from grapes.* • ***You** should wash fresh fruit.*
We can also use **one**, but it is formal: ***One** should always wash fresh fruit.*

Impersonal style

We often use passives when general information is presented in an impersonal way (not intended for a particular person). For example, passives are often used in rules and warning notices ____ , in descriptions of procedures, especially in research reports ____ , and other types of formal written reports where personal reference (**I, we**) is typically avoided ____ .

7 *Twenty students **were given** a test in which they **were asked** to answer 100 questions.*
8 *In the past year, two new computers **were purchased** and some old furniture **was replaced**.*
9 *Parking **is prohibited**.* • *Cars **will be towed** away.* • *Trespassers **will be prosecuted**.*

We can use passives when we want to avoid personal commands ____ and to avoid implying that we are only referring to ourselves or our personal actions ____ .

10 *I can't do all this work in one day.* → *All this work **can't be done** in one day.*
11 *You must remove your shoes before entering.* → *Shoes **must be removed** before entering.*

B Rewrite these library rules using active verbs with *you* as the subject.

Reference books can only be consulted in the library. Special permission must be obtained to use them outside the library. All books should be returned on time or a fine will have to be paid. If the fine is not paid, borrowing rights will be lost. Library books may not be borrowed for others or given to others. If a book is lost, the cost of replacement must be paid.

....
....
....
....
....
....

Reporting in the passive

We can use reporting verbs in the passive when we don't know, or don't want to mention, the speaker of statements and questions ☐ or of orders and requests in infinitives ☐.

12 *We **were instructed** to wait here. • I **was asked** to work late on several occasions.*
13 *I **was told** that everyone had passed. • Some students **were asked** if they **knew** Mandarin.*

We can use reporting verbs in the passive after empty subject **it** to distance ourselves from the reported information ☐. We can use this structure with verbs such as **claim** or **imply** when we are not sure if the information is reliable ☐.

14 ***It is often said** that children can learn foreign languages more easily than adults.*
15 ***It was claimed** that Sandy had stolen something. **It was** also **implied** that he was lazy.*

Note that these passive reporting verbs are followed by a **that**-clause. (NOT *It was reported a problem.*)
Other verbs used in this structure include **allege, assert, hint, report, state, suggest, suspect**

We can use empty subject **it** before a reporting verb such as **mention** in the passive.

16 *Someone mentioned (to me) that he was Peruvian.* → ***It was mentioned** (to me) that he was Peruvian.*
(NOT *Someone mentioned me that he was Peruvian.*) (NOT *I was mentioned that he was Peruvian.*)

We can use a present passive reporting verb plus an infinitive as a way of distancing ourselves from the truth of a current report ☐. We can use a past passive reporting verb plus a perfect infinitive for a report of something in the past ☐.

17 *"The rebels are near the capital."* → *The rebels **are reported to be** near the capital.*
18 *"She inherited a lot of money."* → *She **was rumoured to have inherited** a lot of money.*

We can use a passive reporting verb between **here** and **to be** to report the existence of something.

19 *"There are lots of problems."* → ***There are said to be** lots of problems.* (NOT *There said to be …*)
20 ***There were reported to be** thousands of refugees in camps all along the border.*
Note that **tell** is not used in this way. (NOT *There were told to be thousands of refugees …*)

C Complete these sentences, using appropriate forms of these verbs in combination.

not mention / receive   report / die   ~~request / keep~~   say / be   tell / not use

▶ Dog owners *are requested to keep* their dogs on a leash in the park.
1 There .... more cows than people in some parts of Alberta.
2 The students .... their computers yesterday because of a virus.
3 Mr. Li .... in a boating accident two years ago.
4 It .... earlier, but six more applications .... last week.

D Rewrite these sentences with verbs in the passive, where possible.

People have claimed that they cannot use tasks successfully with beginner level students. I designed the following study so that I could investigate that claim. I created two groups of students, each with different proficiency levels. I gave them a task in which I showed them a set of pictures and I asked them to tell a story. I recorded them as they spoke and then I examined their stories.

....
....
....
....
....
....

Articles and nouns

Nouns are either proper, with a capital letter (**Atwood**), or common, without a capital letter (**author**). Some common nouns are countable and can be singular (**woman, poet**) or plural (**women, poets**). Other common nouns are uncountable and are not used in the plural (**poetry, weather**).

With nouns, we can use an indefinite article (**a** poet, **an** elderly man), a definite article (**the** weather, **the** men), or no article (*We're studying _ poetry written by _ women*).

A Read these statements and choose what you think is the best answer.

1 Igloo building is a skill that was traditionally passed down from one generation to the next.   True / False
2 Igloo building is a common skill learned by all Inuit today.   True / False
3 Soft snow is best for building an igloo.   True / False
4 An igloo should be built as large as possible.   True / False
5 Large blocks should be placed at the bottom of the igloo.   True / False
6 The blocks should be arranged in a spiral.   True / False
7 The completed igloo should be shaped like a cylinder.   True / False
8 Loose snow can be used to seal the gaps between the snow blocks.   True / False

B Read through this text and find

1 another use of the indefinite article *an*
2 a proper noun with the definite article

Building an igloo is a skill that Inuit traditionally passed down from generation to generation. Fewer and fewer people are familiar with the process
5 today, however. Here is a description of how to build your own igloo.

To begin, you will need to locate snow that is firm enough to use as your building material. The snow should also be at least a metre
10 deep. Using a saw, draw a circle in the snow—it should not be too big, or your igloo will be huge. A small, cozy igloo is best.

Use your saw to cut blocks of snow from within the circle. Large blocks will be placed at
15 the bottom, and smaller blocks will be placed toward the top of the igloo. As you build, carve the edges of the blocks to fit together tightly. When you have arranged the first full circle of blocks, carve the tops of the blocks to create a
20 slope. The slope should begin with the first block you placed. Start from the ground and gradually carve upwards around the entire circle, until you get to the final block in the circle—this final block will be the largest,
25 with almost nothing cut away.

Continue placing blocks along the slope you created. This will help you build the igloo in a spiral. Also remember to build toward the centre of the circle to create a dome, not a
30 cylinder. The final piece at the top of the igloo will need to be carved carefully to fit in place.

You can now carve an entrance with the saw. Crawl out the entrance and use the loose snow that surrounds your igloo to seal all the
35 gaps that appear between the snow blocks.

You now have a warm place where you can spend a night in the Arctic!

Articles

We use the definite article **the** with singular and plural nouns.
    1 *The names of **the** authors of **the** books on **the** top shelf begin with **the** letter "A."*

We use the indefinite article **a / an** with singular nouns. Choosing **a** or **an** depends on the first sound, not letter, of the next word. We use **a** before consonant sounds (2) and **an** before vowel sounds (3).
    2 *Have **a** banana! • Is this **a** one-way street? • I need **a** hand towel. • Write **a** "U," then **a** "P."*
    3 *Have **an** apple! • Is this **an** old Volkswagen? • He has **an** honest face. • Write **an** "N," then **an** "O."*

We sometimes use nouns without articles.
    4 *Do you take milk or sugar? • I like pancakes, but not waffles. • Girls are faster than boys.*

The articles **a / an** and **the** are types of determiners. (See page 39.) We can use other determiners (**this, those, my, your,** etc.) instead of articles, but not with them.
    5 ***These** books belong on **that** shelf. • Nora wiped **her** cheek.* (NOT ~~Nora wiped her the cheek.~~)

Nouns

We begin proper nouns with capital letters and use them as the names of people, places, organizations, days, months, and special occasions. Most of them have no article (6). But we use some proper nouns with the definite article in the plural (7) and some in the singular (8).
    6 *William Lyon Mackenzie, Panama, Burnaby, Canadian Tire, NATO, Monday, July, Hanukkah, Easter*
    7 **the** *Chengs,* **the** *Americans,* **the** *Rockies,* **the** *Prairies,* **the** *United Nations,* **the** *Middle Ages*
    8 **the** *Queen,* **the** *United Kingdom,* **the** *CBC,* **the** *CN Tower,* **the** *War of 1812*

We use common nouns to categorize or label people and things. They are countable or uncountable. We can use countable common nouns in the singular, with **a / an** and **each** (9), or in the plural, with numbers and **many** (10).
    9 *Do you have a black **pen** or a **pencil**? • Each **child** should have a **book**.*
    10 *We don't sell **pens** or **pencils**. • There are twenty **children**. • How many **books** will you need?*

We usually use uncountable common nouns when we refer to an abstract concept, an activity, a substance, or a material. Uncountable nouns are not used with **a / an** or in the plural. We can use uncountable nouns with no article (11) and **much** (12).
    11 *Her poem is about **flying**, **freedom**, and bad **luck**.* (NOT *… ~~a bad luck.~~*)
    12 *They have **food** and **clothing**, but they don't have much **water**.* (NOT *… ~~waters.~~*)

C Complete this table with appropriate examples from the text on page 30.

Proper nouns	Indefinite article *a Volkswagen* *an Audi*	Definite article *the Queen* (1)	No article *Panama* (2) ....
Common nouns Countable: singular	*an accident* (3)	*the shelf* (4)	*(by) bus* (5) ....
Countable: plural		*the books* (6)	*children* (7) ....
Uncountable		*the food* (8)	*clothing* (9) ....

Articles: **a/an** or **the**

A Write the numbers of the appropriate examples in the spaces.

A/an or the

We usually use **a/an** to classify people or things when we first mention them ▢ . We use **the** to identify people or things when we think they are already known ▢ .
  1 *We read **a** story about **a** man, **a** young Acadian girl, and **a** priceless diamond ring.*
  2 *Do you remember **the** story about **the** man who tried to steal **the** ring from **the** Acadian girl?*

A/an: classifying

When we classify something, we are saying that it is a member of a category. We use **a/an** when we classify the kind of thing we're describing ▢ or when we want to refer to any example of the kind of thing we're talking about ▢ .
  3 *What's that? ~ It's **a** mouse. • His first movie was **a** comedy.* (NOT ~~His first movie was comedy.~~)
  4 *Do you have **a** ruler? • I'm looking for **a** knife.* (NOT ~~I'm looking for knife.~~)

We use **a/an** when we classify people by the work they do ▢ or the kind of beliefs they have ▢ .
  5 *I'm **a** socialist, not **a** communist. • Isn't your friend Voltra **a** vegetarian?*
  6 *Sheila's **an** architect. • Stanley talks like **an** engineer. • I'm **a** student.* (NOT ~~I'm student.~~)

We can use **a/an** when we classify things in definitions ▢ , in descriptions of particular features ▢ , and with a proper noun for one example of the type of thing mentioned ▢ .
  7 *That painting is **a** Morrisseau. • Have you driven **a** Mercedes? • Is your watch **a** Calvin Klein?*
  8 *The professor had **a** big nose, **a** small mouth, and **an** enormous moustache.*
  9 *Is **a** tomato **a** fruit or **a** vegetable? • **A** dolphin isn't **a** fish—it's **a** mammal.*

The: identifying

When we identify something, we are treating it as already known. We use **the** when we assume that people are familiar with the same ordinary things as we are in our daily lives ▢ and in the physical world outside ▢ .
  10 *Please don't mention **the** sun, **the** sky, **the** earth, **the** weather, or **the** environment today.*
  11 *Where's **the** phone? I left it beside **the** radio on **the** table in **the** corner near **the** window.*

We use **the** when we identify people by their jobs ▢ or their unique roles in society ▢ . We also use **the** with professional organizations ▢ .
  12 *Will you wait for **the** plumber? ~ I can't. • I have to go to **the** dentist. • Ask **the** caretaker.*
  13 *He's thinking about joining **the** police or **the** army. • His brother works for **the** government.*
  14 *Would you recognize **the** Pope, **the** Emperor of Japan, **the** Dalai Lama, or **the** Queen?*

We can use **the** when we want to refer to something as a general concept and we're not referring to a specific example. We do this with inventions and musical instruments ▢ and with people, things, and animals in generalizations ▢ .
  15 ***The** horse was a symbol of freedom to **the** Apache. • **The** customer isn't always right.*
      (= any customer)
  16 *What was life like before **the** computer? • Can anyone here play **the** piano or **the** organ?*

We use **the** when we identify things or parts of things with descriptive phrases after the noun, especially prepositional phrases with **of** ▢ and relative clauses ▢ . We also put **the** before superlative adjectives and emphasizing adjectives such as **main** or **first** ▢ .
  17 ***The** best part was being **the** first person to get in. That was **the** main reason for going early.*
  18 *Can I see **the** book that you bought? • **The** person who called yesterday said you owed him $20.*
  19 *It's **the** middle of June already and I haven't finished painting **the** front of my house.*

B Complete these descriptions with *a*, *an*, *the*, or no article (Ø).

(►) Ø St. Pierre and Miquelon is (►) a group of islands in (1) .... Atlantic Ocean, off (2) ....
coast of (3) .... Newfoundland. You can take (4) .... plane to the islands—they are (5) ....
45-minute flight from St. John's—but you will need your passport. The islands aren't part of (6) ....
Canada. They belong to France, so are a part of (7) .... European Union.

Charlie Chaplin was (8) .... English film actor. He was also (9) .... director. He did most of his
work in (10) .... US. Many people consider him (11) .... greatest comic actor of (12) .... silent
cinema. He appeared in many films as (13) .... poor man with (14) .... small round hat,
(15) .... small moustache, and (16) .... pants and (17) .... shoes that were too big for him,
causing him to walk in (18) .... funny way.

C Choose an answer (a–f) for each question (1–6) and add *a* or *the*.

1 How often have you done this? (...)
2 What exactly is an olive? (...)
3 Where's your dictionary? (...)
4 Why is it so bright outside tonight? (...)
5 What kind of career does Maddie want? (...)
6 What does Mrs. Chauvin's son do? (...)

a It's on .... bottom shelf of my bookcase.
b I think he's in .... navy.
c She'd like to be .... journalist.
d I think it's .... fruit.
e It must be .... full moon.
f Yesterday was actually .... first time.

D Complete this news report with *a*, *an*, *the*, or no article (Ø).

There's (1) .... giant tortoise in (2) .... Galapagos Islands nicknamed (3) .... Lonesome
George who has never found (4) .... mate. Recent studies by scientists suggest that (5) ....
lonely tortoise, now living on (6) .... Pinto Island, actually belongs to (7) .... species from
(8) .... island of (9) .... Española. (10) .... scientists plan to bring (11) .... female from
Española to see if (12) .... George will become interested in mating.

E Correct the mistakes in the use of articles in this text.

I remember/really embarrassing moment when I was starting to learn the English. My teacher's name

was Lee Simpson. He was from London in the Ontario. He was always making the jokes. One day he

wrote words "English Gramer" on blackboard. He asked us if that was correct. Immediately I offered

to answer question. I told him the E should be changed to the A. Lee said that was good answer and

he changed letter. Then he asked me if I was happy with new spelling. With the absolute confidence,

I said that it was now correct. Suddenly, the other students started laughing. I looked around in the

confusion. My friend whispered that it needed second M. "Oh, it should have the M too!" I shouted

out and Lee nodded with the smile. It was correct. But I still remember terrible feeling of the

embarrassment from that moment.

A/an or one, a/an or no article, the or no article

A/an or one

We can use **a/an** or **one** before a noun to refer to a single thing or person.
  1 *This warranty expires after **one/a** year and **one/a** day.*

We use **one** to emphasize the number (**only one** or **just one**) (2) or to refer to a particular but unspecified occasion, usually in narrative (3).
  2 *We only have room for **one** passenger. • He tried to balance on **one** leg, but he fell over.*
  3 ***One** day there was a terrible storm. • **One** time we almost had an accident.*

We use **one** in exact numbers, especially in phrases with larger numbers (4). We use **a/an** in approximate amounts and fractions (5).
  4 *Our laptop cost **one** thousand, **one** hundred, and twenty dollars. • Add **one** cup of flour.*
  5 *That trip cost almost **a** hundred dollars. • It took about **a** day and **a** half to complete.*

A/an or no article

We use **a/an** when we are referring to something as a single unit (6). We use no article when something is not a single unit or it is uncountable (7).
  6 *Would you like **a** coffee? • We have started **a** new research project. • Look! I caught **a** fish!*
  7 *Do you prefer coffee or tea? • He's doing research on fish and shellfish. (NOT ~~He's doing a research~~ ...)*

We use **a/an** before a noun to refer to a single example or instance of a more general thing (8) and no article when we are referring to the general concept (9).
  8 *We bought **a** cheap wine. • I have **an** intense fear of heights. • The elderly man had **a** good life.*
  9 *I hate cheap wine. • Fear of heights can affect anyone. • Life is beautiful, so enjoy it!*

The or no article

We use **the** for a specific meaning (10) and no article for a general meaning (11) before plural nouns such as **dogs** and uncountable nouns such as **money**.
  10 ***The dogs** next door are friendly. • The children have already spent **the money** we gave them.*
  11 *My sister is afraid of **dogs**. • Michelle's boyfriend is always talking about **money**.*

We use **the** with nouns such as **history** or **poetry** when they are followed by **of**-phrases (12) and no article in other contexts (13).
  12 ***The poetry** of Leonard Cohen is popular. • We studied **the history** of Canada.*
  13 ***Poetry** isn't their favourite subject. • He taught us Canadian **history**. (NOT ~~He taught us the Canadian history.~~)*

We can use **the** with nouns to describe a specific time (14) or place (15) and no article with those same nouns after the prepositions **in** or **at** when we're speaking more generally (16).
  14 *That was **the summer** before you were born. • Did you hear that noise during **the night**?*
  15 *After you pass **the school**, you'll see **the church**. • **The prison** is a big red building.*
  16 *Most people would rather be in **school** or in **church** than in **prison**. • I can never study at **night**.*
Other prepositional phrases like this include **at Christmas, at university, in town, in winter**

We use no article in many prepositional phrases referring to general concepts, as in **going by bus**, where there isn't a particular bus being classified or identified (17). We also use no article when we refer to sports (18).
  17 *They came by bus. • Let's go to bed. • Send it by email. (NOT ~~Send it by the email.~~)*
  18 *Anwar loves lacrosse. • Tennis is her favourite sport. • I don't play golf. (NOT ~~I don't play the golf.~~)*

A Complete this text with *a / an*, *one*, or no article (Ø).

(▶) ..One.. time I went out on (▶) ...a... blind date with (1) .... man who had just started working in Vena's office. That was (2) .... big mistake! We went to (3) .... bar. There was only (4) .... free table, in the darkest corner of the bar. He asked if I'd like (5) .... screwdriver. Well, I know there's (6) .... tool called (7) .... screwdriver, but I'd never heard of (8) .... drink called that. He explained that it was made with (9) .... vodka and (10) .... orange juice. I said I'd rather have (11) .... glass of (12) .... white wine. He said he had (13) .... very special white wine from France at his apartment and I would really like it. He gulped back his drink and asked if I was ready for another drink before we left. I said I could only stay for (14) .... drink. When he went to the bathroom, I quickly grabbed my coat and left. Maybe it was called (15) .... "blind" date, but I could see very clearly where it was going. I had to make (16) .... quick exit.

B Using a dictionary if necessary, complete these definitions with *a*, *an*, *the*, or no article (Ø).

(▶) ...A... Christmas tree is (1) .... evergreen or artificial tree decorated with (2) .... lights and (3) .... coloured ornaments in (4) .... people's homes at (5) .... Christmas.
(▶) ..An.. Easter egg is (6) .... egg made of (7) .... chocolate or (8) .... hen's egg with (9) .... painted shell, given as (10) .... present to (11) .... children at (12) .... Easter.
(▶) ..Ø.. Passover is (13) .... Jewish religious festival in (14) .... memory of (15) .... freeing of (16) .... Jews from (17) .... slavery in (18) .... Egypt.
(▶) ..Ø.. Ramadan is (19) .... ninth month of (20) .... Muslim year, when (21) .... Muslims do not eat or drink anything between (22) .... sunrise and (23) .... sunset.
(▶) ..Ø.. Thanksgiving (Day) is (24) .... holiday in (25) .... Canada, on (26) .... second Monday in (27) .... October, and in (28) .... US, on (29) .... fourth Thursday in (30) .... November.

C Complete this news report with *a*, *an*, *one*, *the*, or no article (Ø).

John Millar, who lives near (1) .... Red Deer in (2) .... central Alberta, thought he had found (3) .... bargain when he bought (4) .... Volkswagen for just (5) .... thousand, (6) .... hundred, and sixty-five dollars at (7) .... auction in (8) .... April this year. Everything was fine for about (9) .... month, then (10) .... day, (11) .... car just stopped. John took it to (12) .... local garage where (13) .... mechanic thought there was (14) .... problem with (15) .... gas line. He was really surprised when he discovered (16) .... source of (17) .... problem. He had to remove (18) .... large, tightly-sealed plastic bag from (19) .... gas tank. Inside (20) .... bag was (21) .... wad of (22) .... hundred-dollar bills. It amounted to fifteen thousand dollars. Suddenly, (23) .... Volkswagen was (24) .... even bigger bargain than John had imagined. But John is (25) .... honest man and he reported his discovery to (26) .... police. They are now trying to find (27) .... car's previous owner because they want to know where (28) .... money came from and why it was hidden. John is waiting patiently and hoping that it will eventually be his. When that happens, he won't have to worry about (29) .... money for (30) .... gas for many years.

Nouns: countable, uncountable, generic, pair, etc.

A Write the numbers of the appropriate examples in the spaces.

Countable nouns

Countable nouns can be singular or plural and are normally used to refer to people, animals, and objects ☐, or actions and events ☐ that can be thought of as separate individual things.

 1 *actor, bird, car, child, dog, ladder, man, monkey, mountain, telephone,* etc.
 2 *arrival, crash, goal, lesson, mistake, party, punch, problem, rally, theft,* etc.

Uncountable nouns

Uncountable nouns are used with singular verbs, but not to refer to individual things. They are not typically used with **a / an**. We use uncountable nouns to refer to substances and materials ☐; abstract ideas, qualities, and states ☐; or activities ☐.

 3 *camping, chess, jogging, photography, research, shopping, tennis, training, work,* etc.
 4 *anger, bravery, education, evidence, freedom, honesty, ignorance, love, poverty, safety,* etc.
 5 *alcohol, chocolate, cotton, fur, gas, ink, meat, paint, rice, salt, shampoo, soil, wool,* etc.

There are some uncountable nouns in English such as **advice** or **information** that may have countable equivalents in other languages.

 6 *advice, applause, assistance, cash, equipment, evidence, furniture, garbage, health, homework, information, laughter, leisure, luck, machinery, money, permission, pollution, progress, traffic, violence,* etc. (NOT ~~an advice, a homework, equipments, informations~~)

Countable and uncountable uses

Some nouns can be countable or uncountable. It depends whether we're using the noun to refer to a single thing ☐ or to a substance or general idea ☐.

 7 *She owns **a business**. • I saw **a chicken**. • There's **a hair** in my soup. • Did you hear **a noise**?*
 8 ***Business** is booming. • Do you eat **chicken**? • He has long **hair**. • There's too much **noise**.*

We can also use nouns such as **piece** or **drop** in phrases that are countable ☐ when we want to refer to separate units or parts of nouns that are uncountable ☐.

 9 *Nobody likes having to move **furniture**. • She had **blood** on her sleeve.* (NOT ~~She had a blood on her sleeve.~~)
 10 *There wasn't **a piece of furniture** left in the house. • I could see **drops of blood** on the floor.*
Others like this include **an act of bravery, a hunk of cheese, a bottle of water, a carton of milk, a chunk of concrete, pieces of information, sheets of paper, two slices of bread** (NOT ~~two breads~~)

B Using a dictionary if necessary, complete each definition with one set of nouns (not necessarily in this order) and *a / an* or no article (Ø).

bread / piece / soup / toast   breakfast / cereal / fruit / milk / mixture / nuts
country / government / ~~system~~

Democracy is (▶) ...a system... of (1) .... in which everyone in (2) .... can vote.
A crouton is (3) .... small square .... of (4) .... or
(5) .... fried ...., usually served with (6) ....
Muesli is (7) .... of (8) ...., (9) ...., and
(10) .... dried ...., usually eaten with (11) .... at
(12) ....

Generic nouns

We use nouns as generic nouns when we make general statements about any example (**a** / **an**), the general concept (**the**), or most examples (no article with plural) of the thing we're referring to (11) rather than real or specific examples (12).

    11 *An orange has lots of vitamin C.* • *The telephone rules my life.* • *Women live longer than men.*

    12 *I just ate an orange.* • *Cindy's new telephone is pink.* • *I can see about ten women and two men.*

Pair nouns

We use pair nouns such as **scissors** or **pants** to refer to things made of two matching parts that we use or wear. We usually use them with plural verbs (13). When we put pair nouns after the phrase **a pair of**, we use a singular verb and a plural pronoun (**them, they**) (14).

    13 *These scissors aren't very sharp.* • *White pants don't go very well with black shoes.*

    14 *A good pair of scissors is hard to find.* • *There's a nice pair of pants on sale. You should get them because they're really cheap. In fact, you should buy two pairs!* (NOT ~~two pants~~)

Others include **binoculars, jeans, pliers, pyjamas, shoes, sunglasses, tights**

Group nouns

We can use group nouns to describe a group of people as a single unit, with singular verbs and pronouns.

    15 *The public isn't really interested in what the government is doing unless it increases taxes.*

Others include **audience, band, club, committee, family, jury, majority, parliament, team**

Plural and singular (+s) nouns

Plural nouns are words with distinct meanings that are not used in the singular.

    16 *He said thanks for looking after his belongings.* • *Good manners are important.*

Others include **clothes, congratulations, groceries, outskirts, remains, surroundings, troops**

Plural nouns that do not end with s include **cattle, clergy, people, police, poultry**

Singular (+**s**) nouns are words that end in -**s** and appear to be plural, but are used with singular verbs when we refer to areas of study, activities, and disease.

    17 *Statistics was a difficult course.* • *Aerobics is hard work.* • *Rabies has become a deadly disease.*

Others include **athletics, cards, diabetes, electronics, measles, physics, politics**

We also use singular verbs after some phrases with nouns in the plural describing amounts.

    18 <u>*Five kilometres*</u> *is a long walk.* • <u>*Twenty dollars*</u> *is too much!* • <u>*Two weeks*</u> *isn't enough time.*

C **Using a dictionary if necessary, choose an ending (a–f) for each beginning (1–6) and add these nouns plus *is* or *are*.**

binoculars, clergy, fortnight, mathematics, outskirts, press

1 The .... of a town	a to see things far away.
2 The .... a general term	b the science of numbers.
3 The .... people	c called a .... in Britain.
4 .... described as	d for newspapers and journalists.
5 .... used	e the parts that are far from downtown.
6 Two weeks .... sometimes	f such as priests and ministers.

Determiners

Determiners are words such as articles (**a / an, the**), demonstratives (**this, that, these, those**), and possessives (**my, your, her, his, its, our, their**) that we can use with a noun to help identify whom or what the noun refers to (***That** man with **the** beard is **my** uncle*).

A Read through this text and find

1 another example of *all* with a determiner
2 *all* without a determiner

A My grandfather always drove the car and my grandmother sat beside him. I sat in the back seat, my eyes just below the level of the window, seeing the world through their voices.

5 B My grandfather had learned to drive in the country, where there were few people or vehicles on the road. My grandmother sometimes mentioned that there were a lot of other cars on the road now and he should take a little more 10 care. In reply to this, my grandfather liked to say, "All cars have brakes." He would slow down to turn a corner and we would hear the sound of screeching tires behind us, followed by the loud blast of a car horn. "George, you have to signal 15 sooner," she would suggest. "Oh, what's all the fuss about?" he'd ask. She'd say, "That car could have hit us," and he'd reply, "Oh, all cars have brakes."

C Both of my grandparents had grown up on 20 farms in this area, but during their lifetimes the whole area had changed a lot. They said it was strange that there were no farms now. In place of those old farms were lots of new houses, new streets, and a big new shopping centre. There 25 were still a few old houses with large yards and my grandparents lived in one of them.

D The advantage of all these changes, my grandmother tried to point out, was the convenience of shopping. Everything was close now, even a new 30 grocery store. My grandfather enjoyed the advantages, but he complained about some of the problems that came, he said, from "too many people in too little space trying to do too much at once!" But he really liked the new coffee shop 35 that sold fresh pastries. We seemed to end up there each Saturday.

E It was on our return from one of those Saturday trips that we had our accident. We had eaten some strawberry tarts and my grandfather was telling 40 me how lucky I was that I didn't have to get up every morning and pick strawberries on the farm as he had to. We reached our driveway and turned in. Perhaps his thoughts were back on the farm. Perhaps he didn't expect anyone to be there. He 45 just kept driving up our driveway and straight into the back of another car. There was a terrible crunching sound and we jolted to a stop. A woman appeared beside his window. "Are you okay?" she asked. "Of course not! What are you 50 doing in my driveway?" he demanded. "I was hoping to persuade you to sell your house. Couldn't you stop?" she asked. "You were in the way!" he shouted. "Well, all cars have brakes, you know," she said in a very matter-of-fact way.

B Choose one of the following as the final sentence of each of the paragraphs (A–E) above.

1 There was always someone trying to get them to sell it. (...)
2 As my grandmother turned to see if I was okay, her worried look changed to a smile. (...)
3 He always winked and said it was a special treat for me. (...)
4 I think they sometimes forgot I was there. (...)
5 The circumstances would change, but this answer seemed to cover every situation. (...)

Articles

Articles (**a**/**an**, **the**) are the most common determiners. (See page 32.)
1 *I'm sure I read **an** essay or **a** story by Theroux, but I can't remember **the** title.*

Demonstratives

Demonstratives have different forms before singular nouns (**this**, **that**) and plural nouns (**these**, **those**).
2 *I love **this** chair. • **That** car was speeding. • **These** people were here first. • I forgot **those** papers.*
We can use the same words as pronouns: *Here are the files. **Those** are older. **These** are new.*

We use **this**/**these** when we are referring to things close to the speaker or closely connected to here and now. We use **that**/**those** for things we are treating as further away from here and now. We make this distinction when we refer to times and events (3), places (4), and people (5).
3 *I'm free **this** afternoon. • I'm busy **these** days. • **That** party was great! • I hated **those** meetings.*
4 ***This** classroom is better than **that** awful place we had before with **those** tiny windows.*
5 *Look at **these** people in **this** photo—they're crazy. • Do you remember **that** weird teacher we had?*

We can also use demonstratives to make a contrast between what has already happened (**that**/**those**) (6) and what is going to happen (**this**/**these**) (7).
6 *We discussed the economy last week. In **that** class, we were concerned with money.*
7 *In **this** class, we will shift our focus to politics and the use of power.*

We can use **that**/**those** to add an element of "distance" when we express negative feelings.
8 ***Those** city councillors do nothing but talk. • I never liked **that** old grey carpet.*

Possessives

The possessive determiners are **my**, **your**, **his**, **her**, **its**, **our**, and **their**. We use possessive determiners before nouns (**my seat**), unlike possessive pronouns such as **mine**, which are used instead of nouns and noun phrases.
9 *Are these **our** seats? ~ I think 12A is **your** seat and 12B is **my** seat.* (NOT ~~mine seat~~)
Note that the possessive determiner **its** is different from **it's** (= it is or it has).

We use possessive determiners to express a personal connection to things we own (10), a part of a thing or a person (11), a feeling or thought (12), a family member or friend (13), or an event (14).
10 *I don't know where I left **my** backpack. Can I borrow **your** dictionary for a minute?*
11 *The guard put **his** hand on **my** shoulder. The guard dog just stood there, wagging **its** tail.*
12 *Tasha tried not to show **her** disappointment. She just thanked the teacher for **his** advice.*
13 ***My** wife has invited **her** parents and a couple of **their** friends to **our** son's birthday party.*
14 *When is **your** birthday? • In **our** last conversation, he told me about **his** vacation in Spain.*

We usually use **the** rather than a possessive in a prepositional phrase when we're referring to part of the body of someone already identified. The part is treated as a place, not as a possession.
15 *One man was shot **in the** leg. • Robin leaned forward and kissed me **on the** cheek.*
Note that we say *He kissed **my** cheek.* (NOT ~~He kissed the cheek.~~)

C **Find examples of these determiners with nouns in the text on page 38.**

1 four different demonstratives ....
2 four different possessives ....

Quantifiers

Quantifiers are words and phrases that we use when we refer to quantities that are countable (**a few, many, twenty**) or uncountable (**a little, much**). We can use quantifiers before nouns (*I ate a few cookies and drank **some** milk*), instead of nouns (*Did you want **any**? There wasn't **much** left.*), and with **of**-phrases (*I left **most** of the cookies for you. I couldn't eat **all** of them.*)

Quantifiers and nouns

Quantifiers are words such as **both, most, several**, and **two** and phrases such as **a little** and **a lot**, which we use when we are referring to numbers (*How many?*) or amounts (*How much?*). We can use quantifiers before nouns, like determiners (1), or instead of nouns, like pronouns (2).
1 *There were **two** pies left. • Can I have **a little** sugar, please? • We've had **several** complaints.*
2 *"Let's get **both**," she said. • I don't need **a lot**. • **Most** were about the loud music.*

We use some quantifiers (**a few, many**) only with plural nouns (3), some (**each, every**) only with singular countable nouns (4), and some (**a little, much**) only with uncountable nouns (5).
3 *There are **many** occasions when seat belts save lives, yet **a few** drivers still won't wear them.*
4 ***Each** person has to take a card. **Every** card has a different number.* (NOT ~~Every cards ...~~)
5 *I think the soup needs **a little** salt. • I hope there isn't too **much** traffic.* (NOT ~~too much cars~~)

We can use the quantifiers **all, every**, and **no** with numbers before nouns.
6 ***All six** players were tired. • We get a bill **every three** months. • **No two** people are the same.*

A Complete the sentences with the appropriate quantifiers.

~~all~~, a few, a little, both, each, every, many, much, one, several, ten

1 all, ... are used before uncountable nouns (*money*).
2 .... are used before singular countable nouns (*book*).
3 all, ... are used before plural nouns (*books*).

Quantifiers with **of**-phrases

We can use quantifiers with **of** before determiners (7) and pronouns (8).
7 ***Two of the** students were late. • Take **any of these** chairs. • **Some of my** friends got sick.*
8 ***Two of them** were absent. • You can't take **any of those**. • **Some of us** felt really tired.*
In these structures, there must be a determiner before the noun and *of* before a pronoun.
(NOT ~~Two of students; Take any these chairs; Some my friends; Two them; Some us~~)

We can also use quantifiers plus **of** before proper nouns as place names.
9 ***Most of** Canada will have sunny weather tomorrow.* (NOT ~~Most Canada; Most of the Canada~~)

We usually put **of** between a quantifier and a determiner, but we can omit **of** after **all, both, half**.
10 ***All of these** books are old. • **Both of his** sons play rugby. • I spent **half of the** morning in bed. •
***All these** books are old. • **Both his** sons play rugby. • I spent **half the** morning in bed.*

We can use **every one** (not **every**) and **none** before **of**-phrases (11) or as pronouns (12).
11 ***Every one** of my friends had a cellphone, but **none** of them called me.*
12 *Is there no sugar? ~ There's **none**. • Did you check **every** container? ~ I checked **every one**.*

B Find four quantifiers with *of*-phrases in the text on page 38 and write them in the spaces.

....

C Complete each paragraph with one set of words (not in the order listed).

a / both / each / half   his / my / these / those   his / much / some / the
a little / most / some / seventy-five   a few / our / that / this

I got (1) .... earrings, the small ones I'm wearing, from (2) ....
grandmother. I really didn't like (3) .... green earrings that Andy brought back from
(4) .... trip to Sri Lanka.

Look at (5) .... photograph here in the newspaper. Doesn't it remind you of
(6) .... woman who came to teach (7) .... French class for
(8) .... weeks last year?

Pietro wasn't paying (9) .... attention to the lecture when Angela leaned over and
tapped him on (10) .... shoulder. As he turned, she pointed to (11) ....
notepad and whispered, "Can I borrow (12) .... paper?"

Although there are (13) .... mountain peaks that receive over (14) ....
centimetres of rain annually, (15) .... of Arizona has a warm, dry climate with only
(16) .... rain in winter.

When two horses in (17) .... race finish together at exactly the same time, it's called
a dead heat. It means that (18) .... of them win and (19) .... of them
receives (20) .... the prize money.

D Using a dictionary if necessary, complete these sentences with the quantifiers and the other words.

a few, every, most, lottery, maximum, quota, any, many, much, majority, minority, unanimous

1 A .... is the smaller part of a group, sometimes consisting of only
.... people.
2 The .... weight allowed per passenger restricts how .... luggage
each passenger is permitted to put on board an airplane.
3 A .... system is one that sets a limit on how .... people are
permitted to do something.
4 A .... choice is one that .... person agrees with.
5 In a ...., people can usually choose .... number that they think
will win.
6 A .... decision is one that is based on what .... people want.

E Correct the mistakes in the use of determiners and quantifiers in this text.

I read a newspaper article about some ~~of~~ Albertan boys who got lost while they were hiking in

Newfoundland. One of boys fell and twisted the ankle badly so he couldn't move. Most them stayed

with injured boy while two the older boys left to find help. However, this two boys didn't know where

to go and, after walking round in big circle for a few hour, ended up back with his friends. Luckily,

each boys had brought some water and food with him, so all them managed to survive a cold wet

night out of doors. They were rescued the next day.

Some and any, no and none

A Write the numbers of the appropriate examples in the spaces.

Some and any

We use **some** and **any** with plural and uncountable nouns ☐ or as pronouns ☐ to indicate an indefinite number or amount. We can also use **some** and **any** with **of**-phrases when we are referring to something specific ☐.

 1 *Some students don't get any homework.* • *I wish I had some money.* • *Do you have any matches?*
 2 *I love seashells. I was hoping to find some on the beach, but I didn't see any.*
 3 *Some of the new teachers have already arrived. Have you met any of them yet?*

We use **some** in positive sentences ☐ and in questions or offers expecting positive answers ☐.

 4 *Did you get some new furniture?* • *Can I borrow some paper?* • *Would you like some syrup?*
 5 *Some trees stay green all year.* • *We have some friends in Saint Claude.* • *Let's get some blueberries.*

We use **any** in sentences with a negative element ☐. We also use **any** in questions when no specific answer is expected ☐, in **if**-clauses ☐, and when we mean "it doesn't matter which one" ☐.

 6 *Do Mr. and Mrs. Escobar have any children?* • *Is there any food left?* • *Are there any questions?*
 7 *Ani can't eat any milk products.* • *We never have any free time.* • *He denied any wrongdoing.*
 8 *Any piece of paper will do.* • *Any doctor knows that.* • *Call any time after eight.*
 9 *If there are any problems, give me a call.* • *I asked her if she had any money.*

We can use **some** when we want to refer in a vague way to a large amount or number ☐; an approximate number or percentage ☐; or a person, place, or thing whose identity is unknown ☐.

 10 *It will take some time to recover.* • *They have known about the problem for some years now.*
 11 *He now lives in some village in northern BC.* • *There was some woman here asking about you.*
 12 *That was some twenty years ago.* • *Some fifty percent of working women don't want children.*

No and none

We can use **no** and **none** to emphasize "not any" ☐. We use **no** rather than **not any** before subject nouns ☐.

 13 *There aren't any farms left in that area.* → *There are no farms left.* • *There are none left.*
 14 *No explanation was given.* • *No dogs are allowed.* (NOT ~~Not any dogs are allowed.~~)

We use **no** before singular and plural nouns ☐. We use **none** as a pronoun and with **of**-phrases ☐.

 15 *I had six phone messages, but none from Mr. Brossard. None of them seemed very urgent.*
 16 *When my parents were young, they had no television and no video games so they read books.*

B Choose an ending (a–f) for each beginning (1–6) and add *any*, *some*, or *no*.

1 I don't know what Riyaad does with all his money. (…)
2 I hope you'll be careful when you're using the paint. (…)
3 Do you mind having black coffee today? (…)
4 You have to pick a number between one and ten. (…)
5 I think we'll probably need paper plates and napkins. (…)
6 The concert was good, but I couldn't stay to the end. (…)

a I'll bring ………… .
b I'm afraid there's ………… milk.
c He never has ………… .
d So I missed ………… of it.
e Choose ………… of them.
f Don't spill ………… .

C Rewrite these sentences, adding *some* and *any*. Make any other necessary changes.

▶ Have you had news from your family in Winnipeg? I heard that areas were badly flooded.

Have you had any news from your family in Winnipeg? I heard that some areas were badly flooded.

1 There was woman here yesterday asking if we had old clothes, but I told her we had not them.

....

2 Information in that newspaper article was incorrect. There isn't wolf or bears on Pelee Island.

....

3 I've managed to find dry paper to start a fire, but I can't light it. Don't you have match?

....

4 I'm sure I made mistake when I was typing. If you find mistake, please correct them.

....

D Complete these sentences with *any* (x4), *no* (x3), and *some* (x3).

Did you know that (1) .... thirty percent of students have to leave university, not because they can't cope with their studies, but because they simply can't afford it?

In one survey, researchers found that students cited "(2) .... money" more often than (3) .... other reason such as "courses too difficult" for ending their studies. During interviews with the researchers, (4) .... of these former students said that they had tried to work part-time jobs after classes, but they had discovered that they didn't have (5) .... time or they had (6) .... energy left for studying when they finished their jobs at night.

When the researchers asked these students if they had received financial support from their parents, (7) .... said they had, but the majority said they hadn't received (8) ....

Most of those interviewed said they had (9) .... plans to return to university (10) .... time soon.

E Using a dictionary if necessary, complete the sentences with these quantifiers and adjectives.

any, some (×2), no (×2), none (×2), dead, empty, extinct, scoreless, uninhabited

1 I went to get those .... boxes from the back of the bookstore, but someone else had taken the whole stack. There were .... left.
2 This outport is .... now. At one time there were .... twenty families who lived in this remote fishing village, but nowadays there are ....
3 There may still be .... red squirrels in the forests of Scotland, but there aren't .... left in England. They are certainly .... in the southern parts of England.
4 The last Winter Classic had a lot of great hockey, but .... goals for forty minutes, resulting in two .... periods.
5 Latin is considered a .... language in the sense that there is .... population of speakers who learn it as their first language.

Pronouns

Pronouns are forms such as **it, someone, these, they, them, theirs, themselves**, and **each other** that we use instead of nouns and noun phrases. (*There was a five-dollar bill on the floor of the cafeteria.* **Someone** *must have dropped* **it**. *The boys looked at* **each other**.)

A Read through these short texts and find

1 another example of *it*
2 a sentence with *she*

A I was born in 1939. The other big event of that year was the outbreak of the Second World War, but for the moment that did not affect me. Sydney in those days had all of
5 its present attractions and few of the drawbacks. You can see it glittering in the background of the few photographs in which my father and I are together. Stocky was the word for me.

10 B In the 1940s, a couple of American scientists tried to raise a chimpanzee named Viki in their own home, treating her as a human child. They spent five years trying to get Viki to say English words by shaping her mouth
15 as she made sounds.

C They always say that boys are better at math than girls. When we actually look at the test results, we find that girls generally do better than boys during the elementary school years,
20 but the advantage shifts to boys in high school. That shift occurs when students are given more freedom to select the subjects they will study and girls tend not to go for more math.

D You know the feeling. You meet someone
25 for the first time, and it's as if you've known each other all your lives. Everything goes smoothly. You know just what she means; she knows just what you mean. You laugh at the same time. Your sentences and hers have
30 a perfect rhythm. You feel terrific. You're doing everything right.

E She took his right hand and placed it against hers, palms touching. He didn't get the point at first. Then he realized that she was comparing
35 the size of their hands. The difference made her laugh.
   "What's funny?"
   She told him his hand was funny.
   "Why mine? Why not yours?" he said. "If the
40 difference is great, maybe you're the funny one, not me."
   "You're the funny one," Lu Wan said.
   She matched left hands now and fell sideways to the bed laughing. Maybe she thought they
45 were two different species.

B Choose one of the following as the final sentence of each of the texts A–E above.

1 And you think she's terrific too. (…)
2 They are more likely to choose something else. (…)
3 One of them was exotic and it wasn't her. (…)
4 Handsome was the word for him. (…)
5 Despite their efforts, she never did speak. (…)

Personal pronouns: **I, me, they, them,** etc.

The personal pronouns used as subject pronouns before verbs are **I, you, he, she, it, we,** and **they.** Those used as object pronouns after verbs and prepositions are **me, you, him, her, it, us,** and **them.**

1 *We like **her.*** • ***She** loves **him.*** • ***He** hates **you.*** • ***You** told **them** about **me.*** • *I hope **they***'ll listen to **us.**

When we use a personal pronoun without a verb in a short, informal response, we use the object form (2). The subject form of the pronoun is used after **as** and **than** in comparisons (3).

2 *I'm feeling hungry. ~ **Me** too.* • *Who was making all that noise? ~ **Them,** not **us.***

3 *We don't have as much as **they** (**do**).* • *Both of my brothers are older than **I** (**am**).*

Object pronouns are sometimes used in informal speech: *They are older than me.*

We usually use **it** for an animal. We can use **he** and **she** when we think of the animal as having human qualities or a special personality; for example, when it's a pet or a character in a story.

4 *Pooh is a friendly bear. **He** enjoys eating, singing, and playing with his friends.*

We use the combination **he or she** (rather than **he**) when we are referring to a person who could be male or female (5). We often use a plural noun and **they** instead of **he or she** (6).

5 *By the age of two, **a child** can understand five times as many words as **he or she** can say.*

6 *By the age of two, **children** can understand five times as many words as **they** can say.*

Generic pronouns: **you, we, one, they**

The generic pronouns are **you, we, one,** and **they.** We use **you** for "people in general," including the speaker (7). We use **we** (rather than **I**) to make a statement of opinion more general and to include the reader / listener (8). The use of **one** for "people in general" is formal (9).

7 *If **you** are "self-absorbed," it means that **you** are only concerned about yourself and your own interests.*

8 *When **we** think of cheese, **we** don't usually think of sheep, but as **we** saw in the last chapter, …*

9 *If **one** wishes to be a good parent, **one** should never lose **one**'s temper with a young child.*

In informal situations, we can use **they** to refer to "other people in general" or "people in authority" (10), instead of using a passive (11).

10 ***They** say that an apple a day keeps the doctor away.* • ***They** should keep criminals in prison.*

11 *It is said that an apple a day keeps the doctor away.* • *Criminals should be kept in prison.*

Possessive pronouns: **mine, theirs,** etc.

The possessive pronouns are **mine, yours, his, hers, ours,** and **theirs.** We use them in place of possessive noun phrases (*Marina's room*) (12) and in answer to questions with **Whose?** (13).

12 *I couldn't work in Marina's room. **Hers** is even smaller than **yours** or **mine.** •*
*Marina's parents have a computer too, but I think **theirs** is different from **ours.***

13 *Whose bag is this? ~ I thought it was **yours.** It isn't **mine.*** (NOT *It isn't the mine.*)

We use possessive pronouns in **of**-phrases (**of mine**) after noun phrases beginning with determiners or quantifiers (**a, some,** etc.) (14). We can use this structure to refer to non-specific examples (**a painting of his**) rather than specific or unique examples (**his painting**) (15).

14 *Was Erica a roommate **of yours?*** • *I went hiking with some friends **of mine.***

15 *Tom Thomson was a successful artist. I read that a painting **of his** recently sold for over $50,000.*

C **Find examples of these types of pronouns in the texts on page 44.**

1 two different generic pronouns in one text ....

2 three different possessive pronouns in one text ....

Demonstrative and indefinite pronouns

Demonstrative pronouns: **this, these, that, those**

The demonstrative pronouns, or demonstratives, are **this**, **that**, **these**, and **those**. We use **this**/**these** for things near or closely connected to the speaker (1) and **that**/**those** for things further away (2).
  1 (Picking up a box and some letters at the post office) *This is very heavy.* • *These look like bills.*
  2 (Pointing to the box and letters across a room) *That must have books in it.* • *Those are just bills.*

We can use **this**/**these** when we introduce people (3) and **that**/**those** when we identify people (4).
  3 (Introducing people) *This is Julita Suarez and **these** are her two sons, Nick and Juan.*
  4 (Identifying people in the distance) *That's Ms. Patel and **those** are her two grandchildren.*
We also use demonstratives as determiners before nouns: **that woman, those children**.

We can use demonstratives to make a contrast between what is close in time (**this, these**) (5) and what is further away in time (**that, those**) (6).
  5 *The next question is **this**: who will pay for it?* • *These are the best days of your life, so enjoy them.*
  6 *Philippe and Sandy got married? ~ When did **that** happen?* • *Those were the happiest days of my childhood.*

Indefinite pronouns: **someone, something**, etc.

Someone and **something** are indefinite pronouns. Others are **anyone**/**anything**, **everyone**/**everything**, and **no one**/**nothing**. We use them to describe people (7) and things (8) in a very general way, usually because we can't or don't want to identify them more specifically.
  7 *Someone must have taken my book. Has **anyone** seen it? ~ No one took it. It's over there.*
  8 *The fire destroyed **everything**. We couldn't find **anything** afterwards. There was **nothing** left.*
We can use **somebody, nobody**, etc. instead of **someone, no one**, etc. with no change in meaning.

We usually use **someone**/**something** in positive sentences or questions expecting positive answers (9). We use **anyone**/**anything** in sentences with negative elements or in open questions (10) and when we mean "it doesn't matter who or what" (11).
  9 *I was looking for **someone** who spoke Arabic.* • *Can I ask you **something** about the homework?*
 10 *Can you see **anyone** outside?* • *I didn't say **anything**.* (NOT *I didn't say something.*)
 11 *It isn't difficult—**anyone** can do it.* • *Jeff is really helpful; he'll do **anything** you ask him to.*

Somewhere, anywhere, etc. are indefinite adverbs that we use to refer to places in a non-specific way.
 12 *Let's go **somewhere** different for lunch. ~ But there's **nowhere** within walking distance.* • *I've looked **everywhere** for my glasses, but I can't find them **anywhere**.*

We can put adjectives (13) and **else** (14) after indefinite pronouns and adverbs.
 13 *Do you have **anything smaller**?* • *I think he's **someone important**.* • *There's **nothing new** here.*
 14 *Do you want **anything else**?* • *It wasn't me, it was **someone else**.* • *There's **nowhere else** nearby.*

A Find two sentences containing indefinite pronouns in the texts on page 44.

....

....

B Add these pronouns to the following sentences.

him, his, that, this, they, it, yours

1 Excuse me, Gobi. Is this suitcase .... ?
2 I think .... should cut government spending rather than raise our taxes again.
3 We read a story about Winnie the Pooh and a friend of .... called Christopher Robin.
4 John volunteered to take Ann and Bill's mail, so I gave .... to ....
5 I know we allowed you to go away for a whole month before and now we're asking you to take only two weeks, but .... was last year and .... is now. Things have changed.

C Rewrite these sentences in a more informal style, using *you*, *we*, and *they*.

▶ It is said that one cannot teach an old dog new tricks.

They say you can't teach an old dog new tricks....

1 A person should not use a phone while he or she is driving.
   You know that ....
2 This old factory is going to be demolished so that a new school can be built.
   I heard that ....
3 People who are self-indulgent allow themselves to do or have too much of what they like.
   If ....
4 One should not criticize when one is not sure of one's facts.
   I think that ....

D Using a dictionary if necessary, complete the definitions with these noun phrases and pronouns.

camouflage, a disguise, a mirage, everything, no one, nothing, something (×3)

1 .... is .... you use to change your appearance so that .... can recognize you.
2 .... is a way of hiding .... by making it look the same as .... around it.
3 .... is an effect caused by hot air on roads or in deserts, which makes you think you see .... such as water when .... is there.

E Correct the mistakes in this text.

I studied English in my first school, but I don't remember learning ~~something~~ anything there. We had one teacher who always brought music CDs and she played it for we to learn the words. I think they were hers favourite songs, but in our class no really understood the words. She put us in groups to discuss the songs, but every talked about different something in his groups. And no ones were trying to practise English very much. I only remember the words of one song that went like that: "You can't always get what your want, but if you try sometimes you get what your need." That was interesting words and obviously I did learn somethings from that teacher.

Adjectives

Adjectives are single words (**exciting**, **new**, **thorough**) and compound words (**hard-working**, **well-organized**) that modify nouns. We can use them before nouns (*The **new** teacher has **exciting** ideas*) or after linking verbs such as **be** and **seem** (*She's **hard-working** and her classes seem **thorough** and **well-organized***).

A Read through this magazine article and find
  1 an example of an adverb modifying an adjective
  2 a set of three adjectives before a noun

The ancient Chinese art of Feng Shui has been adopted by modern designers as a way of creating environments that feel comfortable and harmonious. Originally developed as a means of
5 planning the perfect agricultural system in harmony with the forces of nature, Feng Shui has been used for centuries to improve the physical surroundings in which people live and to maintain balance in their lives.
10 Those principles of Feng Shui that are beneficial in the organization of outdoor environments can also be used in the design of areas inside the house such as the bedroom, which is considered to be the most important room in the house.
15 Finding the best position for the bed is very important. The main rule of bed positioning is never to have the foot of the bed directly facing the door. That is what is known as the "death position." Traditionally, the dead were laid out with their feet
20 pointing towards the door to give them better access to heaven. (It also made it easier for the living to carry them out.)
  Ideally, you should position the bed diagonally opposite the door, with the head against a wall, not a

25 window. Avoid putting the bed directly under a horizontal beam that seems to cut across the sleeper. Such a position is believed to cause headaches and even illness.
  Small tables on both sides (not just one side) at
30 the head of the bed help maintain balance, but it is best to avoid cluttering the room with a lot of furniture. Let air flow easily through the space. Those large heavy wooden wardrobes, often with boxes or suitcases stored on top, are a really bad idea.
35 As they tower over the bed, they can make the sleeper feel vulnerable and cause a restless sleep. Do not position tables or other furniture with pointed edges facing the sleeper as their negative energy will cause health problems.
40 The bedroom should be kept as a relaxing space and should not be used for work or as an office. There should be a feeling of lightness, not seriousness, in the air. Blue curtains and bedcovers are more soothing than brown ones. Soft natural
45 materials are recommended. With Feng Shui in your bedroom, you can create a peaceful sanctuary from the stresses of contemporary living.

B Using adjectives and adverbs from the Feng Shui text, complete this summary.

You can use Feng Shui to make your bedroom a sanctuary. Finding the (1) .... position for the bed is (2) .... (3) .... It should be (4) .... opposite the door, not (5) .... under a (6) .... beam, and with the head against a wall. You can have (7) .... tables on both sides of the head of the bed, but avoid (8) .... wardrobes or furniture with (9) .... edges facing the sleeper. (10) .... curtains and bedcovers made from (11) .... (12) .... materials are also recommended.

Emphasizing adjectives

Emphasizing adjectives are restrictive or intensifying. We use restrictive adjectives when we refer to something being special or unique (1). We use intensifying adjectives to reinforce the meaning of the noun (2). We usually put restrictive adjectives before intensifying adjectives (3).

1 *Safety is my **chief** concern.* • *Our **main** problems are financial.* • *Try to give a **specific** reason.*
2 *I haven't played before, I'm an **absolute** beginner.* • *The meeting was a **complete** waste of time.*
3 *The boy was the **only real** hero in the story.* • *Maria got 100 percent, which was the **first perfect** score.*

C Find the two emphasizing adjectives in the text on page 48 and add them to these lists of examples. (One is in the first paragraph and the other is in the third paragraph.)

Restrictive	Intensifying
chief, exact, first, major, only, principal, sole, specific, ...	*absolute, complete, entire, extreme, real, sheer, total, utter,* ....

Describing adjectives

When we use more than one adjective to describe someone or something, we usually put them in the order presented in the table below, with age (**old**) before colour (**green**), etc. Note that this is the normal order, but it is not the only possible order.

4 *I loved that **old green** sofa with the **lovely round** seats and the **big soft** cushions.*

We can often use describing adjectives with different meanings depending on the context.

5 *The Singhs live in a **modest** home near Burnaby.* (= "not very large or expensive")
   *Ruby is a very **modest** young woman.* (= "shy" or "not willing to talk about her own abilities")

D Find one example of each type of describing adjective in the text on page 48 and add it to the correct list below.

Opinion	Size	Physical Quality	Age or Time	Shape	Colour
excellent, lovely, ugly,	*big, huge, long, tiny,*	*dry, hard, hot, light,*	*new, old, recent, young,*	*circular, round, spiky, square,*	*green, pink, red, yellow,*
....	....	....	....	....	....

Classifying adjectives

When we use more than one adjective to classify someone or something, we usually put them in the order presented in the table below, with material (**cotton**) before purpose (**running**) etc. Note that this is the normal order, but it is not the only possible order.

6 *I hate **cotton running** shorts.* • *It's **southern French** style.* • *We found a **Victorian medical** text.*

E Find one example of each type of classifying adjective in the text on page 48 and add it to the correct list below.

Location	Origin or Source	Material	Type	Purpose
distant, indoor, southern, west,	*African, French, Muslim, Victorian,*	*leather, metal, cotton, plastic,*	*economic, medical, scientific,*	*camping, running, swimming,*
....	....	....	....	....

Position and punctuation of adjectives

Position

We usually use adjectives before nouns (1) or after linking verbs such as **be** and **seem** (2).
    1 *I had an **exciting** experience.* • *They faced **enormous** challenges.* • *He has a **kind, honest** face.*
    2 *Don't be **silly**.* • *She became **sick**.* • *They felt **angry**.* • *It got **cold**.* • *He seemed **anxious** and **upset**.*
Note that adjectives are called "attributive" before nouns and "predicative" after linking verbs.

When we use more than one adjective before a noun, there is a typical order. We usually put emphasizing adjectives before describing adjectives (3) and both of these before classifying adjectives (4).
    3 *The weather has been our **principal recent** concern.* • *Her necklace had **real red** rubies in it.*
    4 *Kenya was the **sole African** representative.* • *The **recent economic** news isn't encouraging.*

Some adjectives are typically used after a linking verb, not before a noun.
    5 *The old man is **asleep**. The girl seemed **glad**.* (NOT ~~the asleep man~~ • ~~the glad girl~~)
Others include **afraid, alike, alive, alone, ashamed, awake, well**

In some expressions, we put the adjective after the noun (6) or after an indefinite pronoun (7).
    6 *six feet **tall**, two metres **deep**, two years **old**, notary **public**, the time **available***
    7 *someone **nice**, anything **unusual**, everything **necessary**, nothing **new*** (NOT ~~new nothing~~)

A **In the text on page 48, find two examples of a describing adjective and a classifying adjective used together.**

....

Punctuation

There is usually no punctuation between two or more different types of adjectives before a noun (8). We normally put a comma between describing adjectives in a set of two or more of the same type, especially those representing opinions where the order could easily be changed (9).
    8 *Ken works in a **lovely old Victorian** building. His office has **big black leather** chairs.*
    9 *She likes **wild, vivid, flashy** designs.* • *He was just a **normal, quiet, shy** teenager.*

We put **and** between two colours (10) or between two classifying adjectives of the same type (11).
    10 *I lost my **blue and white** scarf.* • *He wore a **red and black** toque.* (NOT ~~a small and black toque~~).
    11 *She likes **Greek and Lebanese** food.* • *We discussed **financial and educational** topics.*
We put **and** between adjectives after linking verbs: *It's small and black.* (NOT ~~It's small black.~~)

We normally put a comma between the first two adjectives and the word **and** (often preceded by a comma) between the last two adjectives in a set of three colours (12) or three classifying adjectives of the same type (13).
    12 *The flag had **black, green, and yellow** stripes. The tulips were **yellow, orange, and red**.*
    13 *In recent years, the island has experienced **social, political, and economic** problems.*

B **Add commas and/or the word *and* to these sentences.**

1 The flags of Britain and the US both have red white blue designs.

2 He described the wonderful friendly outgoing people who worked in the little Italian cafe.

3 You immediately notice the large plastic vases with pink purple flowers on every table.

4 There are many industrial agricultural applications of the new chemical compounds.

5 What are the cultural religious historic origins of these current regional conflicts?

C Most of these sentences have adjectives in the wrong position. Write correct versions.

▶ I was looking for a plastic little spoon.   I was looking for a little plastic spoon.

▶ There are excellent indoor facilities here.   ✓

1 The soccer entire team played well.

2 The wine made a red small stain.

3 There's new nothing in our cultural main values.

4 You'll need hiking leather comfortable boots.

5 It has a pointed long stem with tiny pink flowers.

6 The windows are in circular wooden huge frames.

7 They are the northern industrial major nations.

8 I love those marvellous new Italian designs.

9 They found a rocking beautiful antique chair.

10 Her alone mother was in the chaos total.

11 The old public swimming pool is closed.

12 We like economic recent Canadian policies.

D Using a dictionary if necessary, add one set of adjectives (in the best order) to each definition.

northern / sharp / cool / thin   prickly / juicy / large / tropical / yellow
similar / white / rare / large / black   bluish-grey / great / hard / shiny white / small

panda: a (1) .... (2) .... (3) .... and (4) ....
animal (5) .... to a bear.
pearl: a (6) .... (7) .... (8) .... or (9) ....
ball that forms inside some oysters and is of (10) .... value as a jewel.
pine: a tree that produces cones and has (11) .... (12) .... leaves
throughout the year. Pines grow in (13) .... (14) .... regions.
pineapple: a (15) .... (16) .... fruit with (17) ....
(18) .... flesh and a (19) .... skin.

E Complete the text with these sets of adjectives (in the best order). Add *and* or
punctuation if necessary.

English older, Italian Greek, big plastic square, great little outdoor, European southern,
Spanish cheap, carefree crazy happy, sour twisted

Some people like to talk a lot about food and the restaurants they go to. I have a friend named
Claude who lectures on (1) .... history at the university. He gets very excited
when he describes a (2) .... cafe in Rome and "all the (3) ....
people" who work there. I also remember listening to an (4) .... woman, who is
a professor of (5) .... literature, complaining about how Spanish dishes are
served in some places with (6) .... wine from (7) .... boxes.
When she speaks about it, her mouth becomes (8) ...., as if she were reliving
the terrible experience.

Adverbs

Adverbs are words (**always**, **really**, **thoroughly**, **totally**) that modify verbs, adjectives, other adverbs, and sentences (*She **always** does everything **really thoroughly** and seems **totally** dedicated to her job*).

Position of adverbs

We usually put adverbs immediately before the adjectives and adverbs they modify.
> 1 *It's **nearly** complete.* • *Is it **politically** correct?* • *She did it **fairly** easily.* • *He spoke **very** quietly.*

When we use adverbs to modify verbs and sentences, we can put them in front or end position of the clause or sentence (2). We can also put adverbs in mid position after **be** or an auxiliary verb (3) and before the main verb (4).
> 2 ***Usually** I have a bagel and orange juice in the morning. I might have a snack **later**.*
> 3 *Some people are **always** hungry when they wake up.* • *I've **never** wanted to eat breakfast in bed.*
> 4 *I **really** prefer to wait a while before eating.* • *I **sometimes** drink coffee.*

Note that we don't put adverbs between a verb and its object. (NOT *I drink sometimes coffee.*)

Adverbs of place and time: **nearby**, **tomorrow**, etc.

We use adverbs of place such as **nearby** and **upstairs** to add information on location or direction (5), usually in end position, and before adverbs of time such as **recently** and **tomorrow** (6).
> 5 *He waited **nearby** while she took the money and went **upstairs**.* • *I slipped and fell **backwards**.*
> 6 *You must leave **here immediately**.* • *I'll be **there tomorrow**.* • *I haven't been **outside recently**.*

Adverbs of frequency: **annually**, **usually**, etc.

We usually put adverbs of definite frequency such as **annually**, **daily**, and **twice** in end position (7) and adverbs of indefinite frequency such as **ever**, **often**, and **usually** in mid position (8).
> 7 *The contract is renewed **annually**.* • *Rooms are cleaned **daily**.* • *I've seen that movie **twice**.*
> 8 *We **often** have to work late.* • *It **usually** rains in the evening.* • *Doesn't he **ever** study?*

Expectation adverbs: **already**, **still**, etc.

We use expectation adverbs to express a connection between events and expectations. We use **already** to indicate that an event is earlier than expected, usually in mid or end position.
> 9 *His plane has **already** arrived.* • *Ms. Palmeri had left **already**.* (NOT *Already Ms. Palmeri had left.*)

We use **still** to indicate that something is going on longer than expected, usually in mid position.
> 10 *We are **still** waiting.* • *I **still** bite my nails when I'm nervous.* • *Jesse **still** avoids crowds.*

We use **no longer** and **not … any longer/anymore** when an event was expected to continue, but did not. We usually put them in mid or end position (11). When we put **no longer** in front position (12), we must use inversion (the auxiliary verb before the subject).
> 11 *It **no longer** works.* • *We could **not** stay there **any longer**.* • *She doesn't live here **anymore**.*
> 12 ***No longer** do the fishing boats come in large groups to catch cod.*

We use **yet** (meaning "up to now") to show that an event is or was expected. We usually put **yet** at the end of questions, negatives, and expressions of uncertainty.
> 13 *Have you read it **yet**?* • *Classes haven't started **yet**.* • *I'm not sure if he's finished **yet**.*

Focus adverbs: even, just, only

We use the focus adverbs **even**, **just**, and **only** to draw attention to one part of the sentence.
14 She was **only** joking. • He can't **even** swim. • Her research isn't **just** about English.

We can change the focus and the meaning when we change the position of these adverbs.
15 Marcus **only** works here on Fridays. (= only Fridays, not other days)
Only Marcus works here on Fridays. (= only Marcus, not other people)

A **Rewrite these sentences. Place each adverb in a more appropriate position.**

1 We thought we had started early our hike, but already other people had left the campsite.

....

2 The workers get paid usually weekly, but they haven't been yet paid for last week.

....

3 Still the students hadn't completed all their work when they had to leave yesterday here.

....

4 Parvita lived recently here, but she doesn't here anymore live.

....

5 We used to hear hardly ever them, but they've become lately noisy really.

....

B **Add these adverbs to the text.**

always, ever, no longer, only, outside, recently, sometimes, today, twice, yet

Actress and model Viviane Tavenard is (1) .... the centre of attention wherever she goes and her appearance in a Montreal boutique this morning was no exception.

But her big smile isn't (2) .... for the crowd of photographers waiting (3) .... (4) .... She's enjoying her life these days and is (5) .... concerned about old romances or bad reviews.

Tavenard has won the Best Actress award (6) ...., but that hasn't stopped her from working on new and (7) .... unusual movies. "This is an excellent time," she said (8) .... in an interview with *Celebrity Life* magazine. "I think that my life is the best it's (9) .... been."

The good news for all you Viviane Tavenard fans is that you may not have seen her best work (10) ....

C **Using a dictionary if necessary, rewrite each of the sentences with one of these adverbs instead of *just*, plus any other necessary changes.**

almost, exactly, now, only (×2), ~~simply~~, very recently

► They just weren't paying attention.   They simply weren't paying attention. ....
1 The couple had just got married.   ....
2 The baby looks just like her mother.   ....
3 He isn't just an athlete, he's a scholar too!   ....
4 Wait for us, we're just arriving.   ....
5 Lunch is just about ready.   ....
6 Wear this crazy hat. It's just for fun.   ....

Prepositions and prepositional phrases

Prepositions are single words such as **at, from, in, of,** and **on** or phrases such as **in front of, next to,** and **out of.** We can use prepositions with noun phrases when we describe people (*a group **of** Italian students*) and things (*the train **from** London*) or when we provide additional information about an action or situation such as the time or place. (***Their** train arrives **at** 4:30 **in** the afternoon. I told them that, if I'm not **on** the platform, they should just walk **out of** the station and wait **in front of** the coffee shop **next to** the main entrance and I'll meet them there.*)

A Read through this text and find another four phrases with prepositions describing time.

The Acadians

Acadians, who can be found in many parts of eastern Canada, are descendants of the first French settlers. Many of these original settlers arrived in the area that is now Nova Scotia during the
5 seventeenth century. Some were explorers, some were traders, and some arrived in the area to begin a new life with their families. The first child born to French parents in Acadia was Mathieu Martin, born in 1636. A number of the children born in Acadia had one
10 parent from France and one from the First Nations; these children and their descendants are called Métis. (Métis have mixed European and Aboriginal heritage.)
   In the 1640s, a civil war broke out between Acadians living in Port-Royal (in what is now Nova
15 Scotia) and St. John (in what is now New Brunswick). This was followed by fighting over the area by the British and the French. At times, this resulted in periods during which no new French settlers came to the area. From about 1670 to the beginning of the
20 eighteenth century, though, Acadians established many settlements throughout Nova Scotia and parts of New Brunswick.
   The British conquest of Acadia occurred in 1710. Acadians were allowed to keep their homes and
25 farms, but they refused to sign an oath of allegiance to Britain. Some Acadians formed militias to fight against the British; this fighting went on for several decades until the Great Expulsion. The Great Expulsion of 1755 was the result of an order by the
30 British that forced all Acadians to leave the area. Some Acadians were deported to other British colonies that are now part of the US, or to France or England. In addition, many fled to the island that is now Prince Edward Island or to New France
35 (Quebec). Thousands of the deported Acadians died as a result of drowning, starvation, or illness.
   A peace treaty was signed in 1763, ending the fighting between the French and the British. After the treaty was signed, some Acadians returned home, but
40 they discovered that the British had given away their land. In order to survive, they became fishermen. The British placed many other Acadians in small groups along the Atlantic coast and the Gulf of St. Lawrence. Some effects of the Great Expulsion
45 lasted until the twentieth century: very few Acadians owned their own land, and they were often dependent on the success of the large fishing companies they had to work for. In the 1920s and 1930s, Acadians formed fishing co-ops through which they helped
50 support each other financially.

B Complete this summary with appropriate prepositions from the text.

Today's Acadians are descendants (1) .... French settlers, many of whom arrived in
Nova Scotia (2) .... the seventeenth century. The settlers came here (3) ....
France to explore, trade, or start a new life (4) .... Acadia. The Great Expulsion forced
Acadians (5) .... their homes; they were sent (6) .... other British
colonies, England, and France. The Acadians were allowed to return home (7) ....
the fighting (8) .... the French and British ended, but they found that their land had
been given away. Many moved (9) .... other parts of Acadia and became fishermen.

Simple prepositions

Simple prepositions are single words such as **at**, **in**, **of**, **to**, and **with** that have a wide range of possible meanings (1). There are others, such as **behind**, **during**, and **past**, that have a more limited range of meanings (2). There are also a few words derived from present participles, such as **following** and **including**, that can be used as simple prepositions (3).

   1 *At lunchtime I went **with** a friend **of** mine **to** a Japanese tea house **in** Essex.*
Others include **as, by, for, from, off, on**

   2 *During the tea ceremony, we had to sit **behind** a huge screen. We couldn't see anything **past** it.*
Others include **above, across, against, before, between, inside, over, through, until, without**

   3 *Following the tea ceremony, we went for a drive. **Including** the drive, the whole trip took three hours.*
Others include **considering, excluding, facing, regarding**

Complex prepositions

Complex prepositions are phrases that consist of two words such as **next to** and **instead of** (4), or more than two words such as **as well as** and **in front of** (5). They all end with a simple preposition.

   4 *Come and sit **next to** me.* • *Could I have coffee **instead of** tea?* (NOT … *coffee instead tea?*)
Others include **according to, apart from, because of, due to, out of, together with**

   5 *There were two or three men **as well as** a group of girls **in front of** me waiting to buy tickets.*
Others include **as a result of, in addition to, in place of, on top of, with regard to**

Prepositional phrases

Prepositional phrases consist of prepositions plus objects. The objects are noun phrases (6) and can include object pronouns (7) and gerunds (8).

   6 *The boy cut the rope **with a knife**.* • *I gave the keys **to the woman** who works **in your office**.*
   7 ***Apart from us**, it was empty.* • *Let's keep this **between you** and **me**.* (NOT … *between you and I.*)
   8 *Some people left **without paying**.* • ***Besides swimming**, I also like hockey and basketball.*

We normally put a preposition immediately before its object, but in questions (9) and relative clauses (10), we often put the preposition at the end. In formal uses, the preposition is sometimes put at the beginning of the question or before the relative pronoun (11).

   9 *He cut it with something.* → ***What** did he cut it **with**?*
   10 *Tanya is the woman. I gave the keys to her.* → *Tanya is the woman (**whom**) I gave the keys **to**.*
   11 ***With what** did he cut it?* • *Tanya is the woman **to whom** I gave the keys.* (NOT *to who*)

Some prepositions are only used at the beginning, not the end, of questions and relative clauses.

   12 ***After** which war was the Treaty of Versailles signed?* (NOT *Which war was it signed after?*)
Others include **above, because of, before, below, besides, during**

C **Using information from the text on page 54, complete these sentences and decide how each preposition is being used.**

a with an object pronoun   c at the beginning of a relative clause
b with a gerund   d at the end of a relative clause

1 Many died .... drowning. (...)
2 They are descendants of French settlers, many .... arrived in the seventeenth century. (...)
3 They depended on the large fishing companies .... (...)
4 The fighting went on until the Great Expulsion .... (...)

Prepositions of time

At, in, on, etc.

We use **at** with an exact point in time.
> 1 *The morning session begins **at** 8:30 and ends **at** noon.* • ***At** that time I was still a student.*

We also use **at** before names of mealtimes or general words for some holidays (2) and when we refer to a person's age as a point in time (3).
> 2 *I'll see you **at** breakfast.* • *What does your family do **at** Christmas?* (NOT ~~at Christmas Day~~)
> 3 *Both my parents left school **at** 16.* • ***At** your age, I was already working full-time.*

We use **in** with a period of time.
> 4 *We usually listen to music **in** the evening.* • *They did all the repairs **in** one day.*

Note that **in the night** ("during a specific night") is different from **at night** ("during any night").

We also use **in** before the names of months, seasons, or years (5), and before phrases identifying centuries and historical periods (6).
> 5 *Spring begins **in** March.* • *It's very dry here **in** summer.* • *Leacock died **in** 1949.*
> 6 *The house was built **in** the nineteenth century.* • *Jazz first became popular **in** the 1920s.*

We can also use **in** for a period of time before something happens or is completed.
> 7 *I'll be back **in** an hour.* • *They said they'd finish the work **in** two or three days.*

We use **on** with a specific day, or part of a specific day, and dates.
> 8 *I'll see you **on** Sunday.* • *The meeting is **on** Monday morning.* • *The exam is **on** May 30th.*

On is often left out: *I'll see you Sunday.*

We also use **on** with special days or occasions.
> 9 *I'll be there **on** your birthday.* • *What do you do **on** Christmas Day?* (NOT ~~on Christmas~~)

We don't usually use **at, in,** or **on** before time expressions beginning with **each, every, last, next**.
> 10 *We had meetings every day last week.* • *I'm leaving next Friday.* (NOT ~~on next Friday~~)

We can use **from** and **to** for starting and end points in time (11). We can also use **past** ("later than") with a point in time (12).
> 11 *The class meets **from** 2:30 **to** 4:30.* • *We lived in St. John's **from** 2008 **to** 2012.*
> 12 *What time is it? ~ It's **past** eight o'clock. Actually, it's already twenty **past** eight.*

A Complete each sentence with one pair of words or phrases plus *at, in,* or *on* where necessary.

Victoria Day / the past	her birthday / next Saturday	six / the morning
four o'clock / Friday afternoon	~~midnight / New Year's Eve~~	sixty-five / 2011
the first of July / 1867	night / winter	September / every year

▶ We all held hands and sang together .at midnight on New Year's Eve.................................
1 I hated the early shift at the factory because I had to start work ....
2 We're going to have a big party for Rachel ....
3 They harvest the grapes ....
4 Because it was so cold in the bedroom, I often didn't sleep very well ....
5 It wasn't as common for people to get time off work ....
6 I can't leave work early because I have a meeting ....
7 Although he didn't think of himself as old, Frank Jones had to retire ....
8 Canada became a country ....

During, for, since

We can use **during** or **in** when something happens at some point(s) within a specific period of time (13). We usually use **during** (not **in**) when we're referring to the whole period of time (14).

13 *We'll be on vacation **during/in** July.* • *The old road is sometimes closed **during/in** winter.*

14 *We need fewer workers **during** long weekends.* • *There were no classes **during** the month of May.*

We can use **during** (not **for**) to describe when something happens and **for** (not **during**) to describe how long something lasts.

15 ***During** April, I'm hoping to go to Calgary **for** a few days.* (NOT *during a few days*)

When we're referring to a period of time up to the present, we can use **for** to describe how long it has been (16) and **since** to indicate when it started (17).

16 *We've been waiting **for** hours.* • *I've been a student here **for** two years.* (NOT *since two years*)

17 *We've been waiting **since** eight o'clock.* • *I've been a student here **since** 2012.*

We usually use a perfect tense, not the Simple Present, with **since**. (NOT *I'm here since 2012.*)

Before, by, until

We usually use **before** very generally for something happening earlier than a certain time (18). We use **by** more precisely when we mean "at/on or before" a specific time (19). We use **until** for a period of time up to a specific point in time (20). We can use **not … until** when we mean "not earlier than" (21).

18 Sanghoon: *Didn't Rob say he would be here **before** six?* (− at some time earlier than six)

19 Jenny: *I think he said he hoped to be here **by** six.* (= at or before, but not later, than six)

20 Sanghoon: *I guess we should wait for him **until** six-fifteen.* (= during the period up to six-fifteen)

21 Jenny: *I bet he **won't** get here **until** six-thirty.* (= not earlier than six-thirty)

In informal uses, **till** is sometimes used instead of **until**: *He won't get here till six-thirty.*

We don't usually use two prepositions together, but the combinations **since before** ("from a point in time earlier than") and **until after** ("up to a point in time later than") are sometimes used.

22 *They've lived here **since before** the school was built.* • *Don't say "Happy New Year" **until after** midnight.*

B **Using a dictionary if necessary, complete the definitions with these nouns and prepositions.**

curfew, deadline, expiry date, after, at, by, during, in (×2), until

(1) .... : the end of a period of time (2) .... which something can be used
(3) .... : a point (4) .... time (5) .... which something
must be done or completed
(6) .... : a law prohibiting people from going outside (7) .... a particular
time (8) .... night (9) .... a particular time (10) ....
the morning

C **Correct the mistakes in these sentences.**

1 I've been waiting since an hour to have a minute with the boss till his next meeting.

2 My sister works as a teacher in Seoul since after 2010.

3 Your application form must be received in this office until 9 a.m. in the first of March.

4 I have appointments in every morning this week, but I can see you on next Monday morning.

Prepositions of place

At, in, and on for location

When something is **at** a place, it is close to it, but not touching it (1). We can also use **at** when we refer to a point on a scale or along a journey (2).
  1 *We'll meet you **at** the bus stop.* • *I think I heard someone **at** the door.*
  2 *Bake the pie in the oven **at** 170°.* • *I'm sure we stopped **at** Moosonee during our trip north.*

When something is **in** a place, it is inside it (3). We can also use **in** when we refer to a place as a general area such as a region or a country (4).
  3 *The money was **in** a box **in** a drawer **in** the desk **in** my office.* • *What's **in** the envelope?*
  4 *Lily is going to spend a week **in** Tuscany this summer.* ~ *Is that **in** France or Italy?*
Note that we say *Who is the small boy **in** the picture?* (NOT ~~on the picture~~)

When something is **on** a place, it is in contact with a surface (5). We can also use **on** when we refer to a place in relation to a line such as a road or a river (6).
  5 *I left the keys **on** the table.* • *She reached over and put her hand **on** his.*
  6 *You'll pass Hanley **on** the way to Saskatoon. It's just a small town **on** the Louis Riel Trail.*

Verbs and nouns with at, in, and on

After verbs such as **shout** and **smile**, we use **at** before an object that is the target of the action.
  7 *Why is that man shouting **at** us?* • *She smiled **at** me.* (NOT ~~She smiled me.~~)
Others include **bark, glance, laugh, look, scream, stare, swear, yell**

After verbs such as **believe** and **include**, we use **in** before objects that describe ideas and things as if they were places.
  8 *I don't believe **in** life after death.* • *The tip is included **in** the bill.* (NOT ~~It's included the bill.~~)
Others include **indulge, interfere, invest, join, meddle, result, specialize, wallow**

After verbs such as **comment** and **concentrate**, we use **on** before an object.
  9 *We can't comment **on** the test results yet.* • *I can't concentrate **on** my work.* (NOT ~~I can't concentrate my work.~~)
Others include **depend, focus, insist, lecture, plan, rely, remark, report**

After nouns such as **ban** and **restriction**, we use **on** before another noun.
  10 *Isn't there a ban **on** pesticides?* • *They have restrictions **on** the amount of money you can send.*
Others include **attack, constraint, effect, emphasis, imposition, limit, perspective, sanctions**

A Choose an ending (a–d) for each beginning (1–4) and add *at, in,* or *on* in each blank.

1 There are restrictions .... travel (...)	a rather than shouting .... each other.
2 Genevieve kept staring .... the goldfish (...)	b of counting the money .... his wallet.
3 They believe .... negotiating quietly (...)	c as it swam around .... its small glass bowl.
4 He was concentrating .... the task (...)	d .... some parts of the country.

B Add *at, in,* or *on* to these sentences where necessary.

▶ Museums in/many small towns rely on/tour buses to bring them customers.

1 The meeting focused economic problems developing countries Southeast Asia.

2 You can either wait the bar or sit a table this restaurant.

3 We were depending my brother to meet us the exit door after the concert.

4 The children were laughing something they had seen a cartoon.

Above and over

We use **above** and **over** to say that one thing is in a higher position than another.
> 11 *There's a full moon **above/over** the mountain.* • *He has a small scar **above/over** his left eye.*

We can use **above** (not **over**) when one thing is at a higher level or point on a scale than another (12). We can use **over** (not **above**) when one thing covers another in some way (13). More figuratively, **above** can be used with the sense of "better than" and **over** with the sense of "more than" (14).
> 12 *It's always colder **above** the snow line.* • *Her name is **above** mine on the waiting list.*
> 13 *There are thick clouds **over** most of British Columbia.* • *I had to wear a scarf **over** my head.*
> 14 *His work is **above** average.* • *Are you **over** 18?* (NOT ~~Are you above 18?~~)

Below and under

We use **below** and **under** to say that one thing is in a lower position than another.
> 15 *Their apartment is **below/under** ours.* • *I keep the bleach **below/under** the sink in the kitchen.*

We use **below** (not **under**) when one thing is at a lower level or point on a scale than another (16). We use **under** (not **below**) when one thing is covered by another in some way (17). More figuratively, **under** can be used with the sense of "less than" (18).
> 16 *Most of New Orleans is **below** sea level.* • *I'm sure the temperature is **below** zero tonight.*
> 17 *The puppy likes to hide **under** the sofa.* • *Do you always wear long johns **under** your jeans?*
> 18 *If you're **under** 18, you can't get into the club.*

We can use **underneath** to emphasize "covered by": *I keep my money underneath my mattress.*

Between and among

We can describe a place being **between** two or more separate people or things (19) or **among** more than two people or things together as a group (20).
> 19 *Find Luxembourg on the map. It's **between** Belgium, France, and Germany.*
> 20 *Find Luxembourg on the map. It's **among** the countries of Western Europe.*

More figuratively, **between** (not **among**) can be used to describe how things are connected (21) and **among** (not **between**) can be used with the sense of "included in" (22).
> 21 *In the study, they investigated the relationship **between** education, diet, and health.*
> 22 ***Among** the advantages of private schools are small classes and more individual attention.*

C **Using a dictionary if necessary, complete these sentences using an adjective or a noun plus one of the prepositions.**

overalls, overflow, overlap, overcoat, overhead, overpopulation, above, below, over, among, between, under

1 I'm wearing a sweater and a jacket .... this ...., but I still feel cold.
2 High birth rates combined with better health care for children are starting to create serious problems with .... some of the world's poorest nations.
3 There is an .... the subject areas of math and physics.
4 The work is really dirty so you'd better wear .... your clean clothes.
5 The number of young children starting school this year is well .... normal and we don't have enough room for them all, so we have to use temporary buildings for the
....
6 A number of people who live near or .... those massive .... power lines say that they have suffered health problems because of them.

Infinitives and gerunds

We use the base form of the verb to create infinitives. We can use the base form after **to** (*I didn't really like* **to read** *when I was younger*) or without **to** in the bare infinitive (*I thought it was torture when the teacher made us* **read** *out loud in class*).

We add **-ing** to the base form of the verb to create gerunds (*Now I enjoy* **reading** *more than anything else*). Gerunds have the same form as the present participles of verbs, but they are used as nouns (**Reading** *is the key to knowledge*).

A Read through this article from an advice column in a magazine and find two more examples of the same verb (*avoid* and *smoke*) being used as both an infinitive and a gerund.

My best friend smokes a lot. I tell her she should quit, but she says she can't. What can I do to help her?

Quitting is hard but not impossible—as long as
5 your friend really wants to kick the habit. "She has a good chance of stopping successfully if she thinks about quitting as a three-part process: she has to deal with her social habit, her psychological dependence, and then her
10 physical addiction," says Lowell Kleinman, MD, a doctor who has helped hundreds of people to stop smoking for good.

Let's start with the habit: when does your friend smoke—on her way to college, after a
15 meal, when she's with friends? Help her break the pattern. "Try going a different way to college, eating at a different place, and avoiding social situations that will make her want to smoke," says Dr. Kleinman.
20 As for psychological dependence: does your friend smoke when she's bored or stressed? Nicotine can have a calming effect, which is why many people continue smoking even though they know it's bad for their heart, lungs, skin,
25 and teeth. Encourage her to avoid stressful situations and to find healthier ways of coping with stress—doing yoga, keeping a journal, or just talking to you.

Finally, physical addiction: when your friend
30 doesn't have a cigarette at regular intervals, does she experience withdrawal symptoms—restlessness, anxiety, irritability, and strong cigarette cravings? If so, her body is addicted. And traditional techniques, like going cold
35 turkey or cutting back gradually, often aren't successful in beating an addiction. Instead, Dr. Kleinman recommends Nicotine Replacement Therapy (NRT)—the patch, gum, or an inhaler—which helps wean your body off nicotine by
40 supplying decreasing doses. The inhaler is available only by prescription, but the patch and gum can be purchased over the counter.

You can also point out that there are real advantages to becoming a non-smoker. She'll
45 not only have better health, but also fresher breath, clearer skin, and whiter teeth.

B Find four phrases in the article above that match the definitions listed here.

1 ....: the unpleasant state that drug addicts experience when they suddenly stop taking a drug; also a way of treating addicts that makes them experience this state

2 ....: performing a system of exercises for your body and for controlling your breathing, used by people who want to get in shape or be more relaxed

3 ....: to stop doing something harmful that you have done for a long time

4 ....: without needing a prescription (written permission from a doctor)

Infinitives

We usually use infinitives (**to** + verb) and negative infinitives (**not to** + verb) after verbs, adjectives, or nouns (1). We can also use them after indefinite pronouns and **wh**-words (2).

    1 *We agreed **to meet** on Friday.* • *I'm happy **to be** here.* • *You made a promise **not to tell** anyone.*

    2 *I was looking for someone **to help** me.* • *I wasn't sure about what **to do** and what **not to do** here.*

We can also use infinitives to express purpose (= in order to): *He only did it to get attention.*

We can use infinitives in clauses with objects, prepositional phrases, and adverbs. We don't usually put adverbs between **to** and the verb (this is called "a split infinitive") unless it is for emphasis.

    3 *We're planning **to take the children to the zoo later**.* • *I want **to (really) understand** Islam.*

We usually leave out the second **to** when we join two infinitives with **and**, or with **or** (4). We can use **to** or **not to** alone instead of repeating a verb or clause (5).

    4 *Brian just wants to **sit and _ watch** videos all day.* • *Do they intend **to buy** a condo **or _ rent** one?*

    5 *Would you like to play?* ~ *I'd **love to _**.* • *I was hoping to go with you, but I've **decided not to _**.*

We don't leave out **be**: *Was Giorgio happy?* ~ *He seemed to be.* (NOT ~~He seemed to.~~)

Bare infinitives

We use bare infinitives (base form of the verb) after modals (6), after perception verbs such as **hear** and **see** with objects (7), and after the verbs **let** and **make** with objects (8).

    6 *I can't **stay** long.* • *What will we **do** if they tell us we must **pay** more?* (NOT *… ~~we must to pay more?~~*)

    7 *I didn't **hear** Tomas **come** in.* • *I've never **seen** anyone **eat** as much as your friend can.*

    8 *Please **make** her **stop**!* • *They won't **let** us **leave**.* (NOT *~~They won't let us to leave.~~*)

After the verb **help**, we can use an infinitive with or without **to**: *Annie helped me (to) clean up.*

Gerunds

We can use gerunds (verb + **-ing**) and negative gerunds (**not** + verb + **-ing**) after verbs and prepositions (9). We can also use gerunds as subjects (10).

    9 *I don't mind **waiting**.* • *Andrea enjoys **not having** a job.* • *She watches TV **instead of working**.*

    10 ***Studying** makes me sleepy.* • *My doctor says that **swimming** is the best kind of exercise.*

Gerunds are also called **-ing** forms. They are often used after **No** on signs: *No Parking.*

We can use gerunds in clauses with objects, prepositional phrases, and adverbs (11). Before gerunds, we can use nouns (**Kim**) or object pronouns (**them**), but possessive nouns and determiners (**Tom's**, **their**) can also be used, typically in formal situations (12).

    11 *He denied **taking the money**.* • *They recommend **washing silk shirts gently in cold water**.*

    12 *I can't recall **Kim/Kim's** visiting us.* • *We listened to **them/their arguing** all night.*

Gerund or present participle?

We use gerunds like nouns, which can be subjects or objects (13). We usually use present participles as verbs with different forms of **be** (14). We use present participles, not gerunds, in reduced versions of relative clauses or adverbial clauses (15).

    13 ***Talking** and acting are two very different things.* • *Have they finished **(the) cleaning** yet?*

    14 *We **were talking** about money.* • *I **have been cleaning** my room all morning.*

    15 *The man (who is) **talking** to Liz is her dad.* • *While (I'm) **cleaning**, I listen to music.*

C **Look at the four definitions listed in part B at the bottom of page 60 and find one example of each of the following:**

1 an infinitive after a verb ....   2 a bare infinitive after a verb ....

3 a gerund after an infinitive ....   4 a gerund after a preposition ....

Verbs with infinitives and gerunds

Verbs used with infinitives only

We use infinitives, not gerunds, after verbs such as **hope** and **offer** (1). After verbs such as **invite** and **tell**, we must include a noun or object pronoun to identify the subject before the infinitive (2). After verbs such as **ask** and **want**, we can include the subject of the infinitive or leave it out if it's the same as the subject of the verb (3).

1 *I'm **hoping to get** a day off soon. • We **offered to pay** for the damage.* (NOT ~~offered paying~~)
2 *They **told me not to wait** for them. • Adeel **invited us to go** with him.* (NOT ~~invited to go~~)
3 *I **asked Sam to stay**. I **wanted him to wait**, but he **wanted to leave** right away.*

Verbs used with gerunds only

After verbs such as **avoid** and **enjoy**, we use gerunds, not infinitives (4). After verbs such as **imagine** and **mind**, we can include a noun or object pronoun before the gerund (5). We put gerunds after verbs with prepositions such as **concentrate on** and after phrasal verbs such as **give up** (6).

4 ***Avoid eating** doughnuts and candy. • We **enjoy travelling** by train.* (NOT ~~enjoy to travel~~)
5 *I **imagined Jenny walking** on a sunny beach. • Would you **mind us waiting** outside?*
6 *He should **concentrate on studying**, not **singing**. • Have you **given up exercising** already?*

Verbs used with infinitives or gerunds

After **begin**, **continue**, **intend**, and **start**, we can usually use either infinitives or gerunds with little difference in meaning.

7 *Josh **started to eat/eating** the soup, but it was very spicy. He **began to cough/coughing**.*
We use infinitives after present participles: *Is it starting to snow?* (NOT ~~Is it starting snowing?~~)

After **hate**, **like**, **love**, and **prefer**, we can usually use infinitives or gerunds with little difference in meaning (8). When we are referring to an activity in general (not performed by the subject), we use a gerund (9). After **would hate/like/love/prefer** we use infinitives (10).

8 *Katy **loves to play/playing** the piano. • Don't you **prefer to study/studying** at home?*
9 *I **hate wrestling** because it's so violent. It shouldn't be on TV. I don't **like boxing** either.*
10 ***Would** you **like to come** with us? • I'd **love to see** you tonight.* (NOT ~~I'd love seeing you tonight.~~)
Note the use of **would rather** + bare infinitive: *I'd rather stay here.* (NOT ~~I'd rather to stay here.~~)

After **advise**, **allow**, **encourage**, and **permit**, we can use a noun or object pronoun as the subject of the infinitive. When there is no subject, we use the gerund for an activity in general.

11 *They don't **allow us to drink**. • They don't **allow drinking**.* (NOT ~~They don't allow us drinking.~~)

After **feel**, **hear**, **see**, and **watch**, we can use a noun or object pronoun as the subject with a bare infinitive for a single or completed action and with a gerund for a repeated or continuous action.

12 *When I rang the doorbell, I **heard** a dog **bark**. • Did you **hear** that dog **barking** last night?*
When there is no subject, we use a gerund: *I also heard shouting.* (NOT ~~I also heard shout.~~)

After **forget**, **regret**, **remember**, and **stop**, we use infinitives for actions that will happen later (13) and gerunds for actions that have already happened (14).

13 ***Remember to take** an umbrella.* (when you go out later) *• I **regret to inform** you about this.* (I'm going to inform you)
14 *Don't you **remember taking** it?* (when you left earlier) *• I **regret saying** that.* (I said it earlier)

After **need**, we often use an infinitive, but we can use a gerund with the same meaning as the passive infinitive (15). We can use **mean** with an infinitive (= intend) or **mean** with a gerund (= result in) (16). We can use **try** with an infinitive (= make an effort) or **try** with a gerund (= experiment with) (17).

15 *I **need to do** some laundry. • These towels **need washing**. (= These towels **need to be washed**.)*
16 *I **meant to ask** you about your new job. Will it **mean spending** more time away from home?*
17 *I must **try to get** to work on time tomorrow. I think I'll **try setting** my alarm a bit earlier.*

A Add one pair of verbs to each sentence in the table, with the first verb in an appropriate form and the second verb as an infinitive or a gerund.

enjoy / take, hope / visit, imagine / make, invite / stay, love / be, want / spend

1 **Verb + infinitive.** I .... Japan next summer.
   Others include **agree, aim, apply, decide, demand, fail, offer, plan, refuse, vote**

2 **Verb + noun / object pronoun + infinitive.** My friend Ryoko has .... me
   .... with her.
   Others include **command, convince, force, instruct, order, persuade, remind, tell, tempt, urge**

3 **Verb (+ noun / object pronoun) + infinitive.** She .... me .... a
   whole month there.
   Others include **ask, beg, expect, wish**

4 **Verb + gerund.** She says she'll .... me to all her favourite places.
   Others include **admit, avoid, consider, deny, finish, give up, mention, practise, recommend, suggest**

5 **Verb (+ noun / object pronoun) + gerund.** I can .... her .... plans
   already.
   Others include **celebrate, detest, dislike, involve, keep, mind, miss, prevent, recall, resent**

6 **Verb + infinitive or gerund.** I would .... able to go sooner.
   Others include **begin, continue, forget, hate, like, learn, mean, regret, remember, try**

B Add appropriate forms of the verbs from each set to each sentence.

allow / take, avoid / try / drive, force / stop / play, forget / send, mean / clean, prefer / not talk

1 My teachers would never .... students .... the exams home.
2 Don't .... me a postcard when you go to Japan.
3 I'm sorry about the mess. I .... up before you came back.
4 Most people .... about how much money they have or earn.
5 We usually .... through the centre of town during rush hour.
6 Bad weather .... us .... tennis earlier today.

C Correct the mistakes in the use of infinitives and gerunds in this text.

I have never forgotten ~~work~~ working as a hotel maid one summer when I was a teenager. My aunt was an

assistant manager at the hotel and she encouraged me take the summer job. She had been a maid

at one time and she advised me remember clean the bathrooms really well. Nobody likes clean

bathrooms, but I didn't mind do it as part of my summer job. That's when I was first starting learn

English. Some of the visitors were really nice and I could practise speak English with them. I enjoyed

try improve my English and it helped me when I went to college later. I also learned that I didn't

want work as a hotel maid forever, but I don't regret do it for one summer. I decided study harder

at school so I could go to college and try get a better job.

Reporting

We can report what someone says by repeating the original words of the speaker (*He said, "I'm sorry."*). This is called direct speech. When we don't need or want to repeat the actual words of the speaker, we can use indirect speech (*He said that he was sorry*) or a summary report (*He apologized*).

A **Read through this text and find two more sentences containing the verb *say* used with**

1 direct speech
2 indirect speech

A On Sunday afternoons my grandmother used to take me with her to visit Mr. Calum Mackenzie. My grandmother and Mrs. Mackenzie, his wife, had been good friends and had gone for walks together every Sunday. When Mrs. Mackenzie died, my grandmother was one of the women who helped Mr. Mackenzie and she still liked to visit him, even on the coldest winter days.

B Mr. Mackenzie was, as my grandmother put it, "a man of few words." This probably wasn't obvious to everyone because, when we arrived, he would always call out, "Well, hello there!" and give us a big smile like a friendly neighbour ready to stop and chat. But I never saw him talking to any of the neighbours. I remember one time my grandmother commented that maybe he didn't speak much because he didn't hear as well as he used to. Mr. Mackenzie turned in his chair. "Maybe I don't hear anything worth talking about," he grumbled.

C My grandmother would tell him about everything that had been going on in town as she walked around the house picking things up and putting them away. The news would be served with the tea and cookies we always had with him on Sundays. From the outside, it would have sounded as if we were all having a lively conversation, punctuated by the sound of teaspoons clinking on saucers.

D When we cleared the tea things away and my grandmother disappeared into the kitchen, a silence would fall over the living room. I would sit quietly with Mr. Mackenzie and stare into the glowing embers of the open fire. He would cut up chunks of black tobacco and put them in his pipe and light it. He'd puff away with his eyes almost closed as the sweet smell filled the warm room.

E In my English class we had read a story about the poets Wordsworth and Coleridge. One time Wordsworth went to visit Coleridge at his cottage. He walked in, greeted his friend, and sat down. He didn't say another word for three hours. Nor did Coleridge. Then Wordsworth got up and, as he was leaving, thanked Coleridge for a perfect evening. The teacher asked us what we thought about the story and those who had opinions mostly said that it was a strange story or impossible or that poets must be weird people. I didn't say anything.

F When we eventually got ready to leave, my grandmother would give Mr. Mackenzie advice about eating and his health. He would just nod and say, "Thanks for coming by," in a voice that told us he had had a perfect afternoon.

B **Choose one of the following as the final sentence of each of the paragraphs (A–F) above.**

1 But it was really only my grandmother who was talking. (...)
2 We could easily spend an hour like that. (...)
3 He didn't say much, but he obviously wasn't deaf. (...)
4 It always felt so much colder when we left. (...)
5 She said we were going "just to see how Calum is doing". (...)
6 It didn't seem strange to me and I knew it wasn't impossible. (...)

Direct speech

We usually put direct speech in quotation marks after a reporting verb such as **reply** or **say**.

1 *Francisco said,* **"I need you here."** *Dorothy replied,* **"I can't come before next weekend."**

We can also put the reporting verb with its subject after direct speech (2) or in the middle of two parts of direct speech (3).

2 **"That's too late,"** *he said.* **"Well, that's just too bad,"** *she told him and put the phone down.*

3 **"Hi,"** *he began.* **"It's me again. I was wondering,"** *he continued,* **"if we could start over."**

After direct speech, the reporting verb is sometimes put before its subject in the reporting clause (4), but not when the subject is a pronoun (5).

4 **"We will never give up,"** *shouted one of the demonstrators as he was dragged away.*

5 **"Where's Tim?"** *he asks impatiently.* **"Not here yet,"** *she replies.* (NOT ~~replies she~~)

Direct speech is sometimes reported in parentheses (6), or after a colon (7), without a reporting verb. We can also use direct speech to report thoughts and reactions as if they had been spoken (8).

6 *Blythe Danner didn't want her daughter to be an actress (**"I thought she was too bright"**).*

7 *Gwyneth Paltrow never had any doubts:* **"I always knew what I wanted to do."**

8 *I suddenly realized* **"I hate him!"** *Then I thought* **"Oh, no!"** *when I remembered that kiss.*

We use quotation marks when we want to report exactly a specific word, phrase, or title of a short work (9). We put single quotation marks around direct speech that is quoted within another piece of direct speech (10).

9 *There was a sign with* **"No Entry"** *printed in big red letters. • Have you heard the song* **"Heart of Gold"**?

10 *She said,* "I heard someone whisper **'Jan'** and I turned, but no one was there."

C Find an example of each of the following in the text on page 64:

1 A reporting verb (not **say**) before direct speech: ....

2 A reporting verb after direct speech: ....

D Using examples 1–3 above as a guide, complete these punctuation rules with the words *comma* or *quotation marks*.

After the reporting verb, before direct speech, we put the (1) .... before the (2) .... After direct speech, before the reporting verb plus subject, we put the (3) .... before the (4) .... When the reporting verb plus subject is in the middle of two parts of direct speech, we use (5) .... to close the first part and (6) .... to open the second part.

E Add appropriate punctuation to this text.

Karen Ms. Lee called out I'd like you to come and meet Michael a girl appeared in the doorway how do you do she said nice to meet you he mumbled please don't call him Michelle or Mikey or any other silly names warned Ms. Lee as she swept out of the room look I drew a picture of the bear from Goldilocks Karen suddenly said what one he asked oh no you little Mickey Mouse she said as she came into the room you must say which one not what one if you're going to survive here

Indirect speech

We use indirect speech (or reported speech) to report the meaning of what was said, not the exact words. We put indirect speech in a noun clause beginning with **that** (1) or a **wh**-word (**what, where, when,** etc.) (2). In informal uses, we often omit **that**.

1 "It's a strange story." → *They said **(that) it was a strange story.***
2 "What do you think about the story?" → *The teacher asked us **what we thought about the story.***

Words for places, times, and people in indirect speech

In indirect speech, we change those words that refer to the speaker's situation (**I, my, this**) to words that reflect the different point of view of the person reporting (**she, her, that**).

3 "**I** don't like **my** hair in **this** style." → *She said **she** didn't like **her** hair in **that** style.*

We usually change words that refer to the place of speaking (4) and the time of speaking (5) to reflect the point of view of the person reporting.

4 "Wilfrid Laurier lived **here**, but not in **this** particular house." → *The tour guide explained that Wilfrid Laurier had lived **there**, but not in **that** particular house.*
5 "It rained **yesterday** and most of **last week**." → *The man pointed out that it had rained **the day before** and most of **the previous week**.*

Note also: "now" → **then**, "tomorrow" → **the next day**, "two days ago" → **two days earlier**

We also change pronouns to reflect the different point of view of the person reporting.

6 "**We** fixed it **ourselves**." → *The boys claimed that **they** had fixed it **themselves**.*
7 Pierre said to Veronica, "I'll give **you my book**." → *Pierre said that **he** would give **her his book**.*
8 Sandra said to me, "I'll give **you my book**." → *Sandra said that **she** would give **me her book**.*

Tense in indirect speech

After a reporting verb in the Simple Past, we usually change Simple Present to Simple Past (9) and Present Perfect to Past Perfect (10).

9 "It **is** late and I **have** a headache." → *She complained that it **was** late and she **had** a headache.*
10 "I've heard that they **have** been arguing." → *He said he'd heard that they **had** been arguing.*

We can report Simple Past speech using the Simple Past or change it to Past Perfect to emphasize that the event was earlier in the past.

11 "I **didn't see** Mark." → *He said he **didn't see** Mark.* (OR *He said he **hadn't seen** Mark.*)

We can use the Simple Present after reporting verbs in the Simple Present for current (12), future (13), or permanent (14) situations. After a reporting verb in the past, we sometimes use a verb in the present for a situation that has not changed (15).

12 "Business **is** good and profits **are** up." → *Delco reports that business **is** good and profits **are** up.*
13 "It **is** going to be very cold." → *The meteorologist says that it **is** going to be very cold.*
14 "My parents **live** in Bermuda." → *She likes to tell everyone that her parents **live** in Bermuda.*
15 "I **love** you." → *He said he **loves** me.*

Modals in indirect speech

We usually change the modals **can** (→ **could**), **may** (→ **might**), and **will** (→ **would**) in indirect speech.

16 "You **can** go." → *He said we **could** go.* • "I'll wait." → *She said that she **would** wait.*

We don't change **could, might, ought to,** or **should** from direct to indirect speech.

We change **will / shall** to **would** in predictions (17) and we change **shall** to **should** in offers or suggestions (18).

17 "I **will** do it right away." → *I remember she said that she* ***would*** *do it right away.*
18 "**Shall** I close the door?" → *The new student asked if he* ***should*** *close the door.*

We can use **must** or **had to** when we report that something was necessary.
  19 "You **must** do more." → *He said we* ***must*** *do more.* OR *He said we* ***had to*** *do more.*

A Complete each reporting sentence in such a way that it is as similar as possible in meaning to the direct speech above it.

1 "I left my jacket here yesterday."
  He said that ....

2 "This new book is the funniest thing I've ever read."
  The reviewer wrote that ....

3 "We won't eat it now, but we may have it for lunch tomorrow."
  She said that ....

4 "You should take as much water as you can carry."
  He advised us that ....

5 "I must get something to eat or I'll faint."
  You told me that ....

6 "Demand for new computers in Canada is declining."
  CompCo is reporting that ....

7 "Shall I get rid of these old boxes in the closet?"
  She asked if ....

B Complete the text with these verbs.

are, is, has, live, can, can't, will, were, was, had, lived, could, won't, would

When she died at the age of 122, Jeanne Calment was the oldest person on record. This amazing woman, from Arles in France, had not exactly lived what might be described as "a healthy lifestyle." Family and friends reported that she (1) .... fond of cheese, wine, and chocolate. She had also smoked cigarettes until she was 117. We asked several experts how a person, especially a cigarette smoker, (2) .... live so long. They offered more than one answer. "The average life expectancy (3) .... now about 80 for women and 75 for men," observed Dr. Elizabeth Jones, director of the Centre for Studies on Aging. She says that there (4) .... been a steady rise in the maximum age of death throughout Europe during the past century and a major reason for this is improved medical care. Another researcher, Dr. Michael Glass, says, "There (5) .... no theoretical reasons why we (6) .... have a life span of 200 years." Better medical care (7) .... be the only factor, according to Dr. Glass. He explained that genetic engineering (8) .... soon allow us to repair or replace damaged cells, the real cause of aging. He believes that we (9) .... be able to stop the aging process. Other researchers have noted that attitude is also an important factor in longer life. Dr. John Park is the author of *Living Beyond 100*. "Those who (10) .... to a ripe old age," he says, "are those who (11) .... cope with stress and other difficulties in life." He wrote in his bestselling book that people who (12) .... past 100 (13) .... almost always optimistic and (14) .... a great attitude toward life.

Reporting verbs

Reporting verbs with **that**-clauses

We use verbs such as **mention** or **say** as reporting verbs before **that**-clauses with indirect speech.

    1 "I've been sick." → *She **mentioned that** she'd been sick.* • "It's cold." → *Kara **said that** it was cold.*

After reporting verbs such as **tell** and **assure**, we must include an object (the hearer) before a **that**-clause.

    2 "She has gone home." → *He **told me that** she had gone home.* (NOT ~~He told that she had gone home.~~)

    3 "You will be paid." → *I **assured them that** they would be paid.* (NOT ~~I assured that they …~~)

Other verbs used like this include **convince, inform, notify, persuade, remind, warn**

After a reporting verb such as **say**, we can use **to** + object before a **that**-clause (4). After a reporting verb such as **agree**, we use **with** + object before a **that**-clause (5).

    4 "I'm not ready." → *He **said (to me) that** he wasn't ready.* (NOT ~~He said me that he wasn't ready.~~)

Other verbs used like this include **admit, confess, mention, propose, report**

    5 "You're right. There is a mistake." → *He **agreed (with me) that** there was a mistake.*
      (NOT ~~He agreed me that there was a mistake.~~)

Other verbs used like this include **argue, check, confirm, disagree**

Reporting verbs with infinitives and gerunds

After reporting verbs such as **invite** and **encourage**, we include an object before an infinitive.

    6 "You can go with me." → *He **invited us to go** with him.* (NOT ~~He invited us that we could go.~~)

    7 "You shouldn't quit." → *She **encouraged me not to quit**.* (NOT ~~She encouraged not to quit.~~)

Other verbs used like this include **ask, expect, order, remind, urge, warn**

After a reporting verb such as **offer**, we don't include an object before an infinitive.

    8 "I'll help you later." → *He **offered to help** us later.* (NOT ~~He offered us to help us later.~~)

Other verbs used like this include **apply, decide, decline, demand, refuse, volunteer**

After a reporting verb such as **promise**, we can use an infinitive or a **that**-clause.

    9 "I'll fix it." → *He **promised to fix** it.* OR *He **promised that he would fix** it.*

Other verbs used like this include **agree, claim, hope, propose, threaten, vow**

After reporting verbs such as **deny** and **suggest**, we can use a gerund or a **that**-clause.

    10 "I didn't take it." → *She **denied taking it**.* OR *She **denied that she had taken it**.*

    11 "You should leave." → *He **suggested leaving**.* OR *He **suggested that they should leave**.*
      (NOT ~~He suggested them leaving. He suggested them to leave. He suggested to leave.~~)

Other verbs used like this include **admit, mention, propose, recommend, report**

Reporting verbs in summary reports

We can use some reporting verbs to summarize what was said (12). Some verbs, such as **speak, talk,** and **thank**, are only used in summary reports, not with direct or indirect speech (13).

    12 "Don't come back—or else!" → *They **threatened** us.* • "It was me. I did it." → *He **confessed**.*

    13 *He **talked** to Kevin about the problem.* • *She **spoke** briefly to reporters.* • *I **thanked** them.*
      (NOT ~~He talked to me, "Hi, how are you?"~~ • ~~She spoke to us that she liked it.~~)

We can use reporting verbs such as **boast** or **lie** with **about** to create a summary report.

    14 "I beat everyone. I'm the best!" → *He **boasted about** his win.* • *He **lied about** how he did it.*

Other verbs used like this include **complain, explain, inquire, joke, protest, speak, write**

A Complete each sentence in such a way that it is as similar as possible in meaning to the sentence above it.

1 "Mr. Jawal, there's something wrong with the lights."
I mentioned ....

2 "Julia, you and your friends have to clean up after the party."
I reminded ....

3 "Don't touch any of the wires."
He warned ....

4 "I didn't do anything wrong."
He denied ....

B Complete the text with appropriate forms of these reporting verbs.

ask, beg, claim, explain, mention, shout, talk, tell, think, wonder

I was in the Arctic last summer to photograph foxes, but I had been having no luck. I was on my way home one day when I saw a construction engineer named Anguta Mitsuk waving and (1) .... to me as I drove by. We had met the previous weekend and he (2) .... some areas further north where I might find foxes. I (3) .... why he was trying to stop me there. I pulled over and got out to (4) .... to him. He (5) .... if I was still looking for foxes.

We walked over to what was left of some old rusted cars by the side of the road. I looked down and saw three little foxes asleep beside a broken car door. He (6) .... me that he would have to catch them all and move them away from there. It was his next construction site, he (7) .... "I'm afraid that when we (8) .... that we are 'developing' or 'improving' an area, we don't always make things better for wild animals."

"Let me get my camera and take some photos before you do anything," I (9) .... him. I ran to get my camera. I do hope they'll survive, I (10) .... to myself.

That afternoon I took nearly one hundred photos while the young foxes played among the old cars.

C Correct the mistakes in this text.

The word "biker" is used to describe people who ride motorcycles. They sometimes ride around in gangs. Some people say me that bikers are dangerous criminals, but I can't agree them that all bikers are like that. One time I had a flat tire on the highway and two bikers in black leather jackets stopped and offered me to help. I explained them that I can't get the wheel off. One of them told that it was "no problem" and assured that it wouldn't take long. He even suggested me to stand behind the car for safety and warned me watch out for broken glass on the ground. They fixed it really quickly and joked the small wheels on my little car. I spoke them thanks. They refused take any money when I offered pay them. They were like angels. Actually, it said on their jackets that they were "Hell's Angels."

That-clauses and wh-clauses

A noun clause (or nominal clause) is a clause we can use like a noun or noun phrase as the object of a verb. We can introduce noun clauses with **that** (*I'm hoping **that the weather is going to be nice this weekend***), a **wh**-word (*Do you know **what the forecast is?***), and **if** or **whether** (*I was wondering **if/whether we might be able to have a picnic on Sunday***).

A Read through this text and find

1 another sentence containing two noun clauses beginning with *that*
2 a sentence containing a noun clause beginning with *if* or *whether*

According to one old song, love and marriage go together like a horse and carriage. These days, however, a long-lasting marriage may be almost as hard to find as a horse and carriage on our busy streets. Statistically, it is now more likely that a marriage will end in divorce than continue in a loving relationship. It makes you wonder if getting married is worth the effort.

Is it simply the case that marriage has become a gamble with less than a 50 percent chance of success? Not really, say researchers at the Newport Institute, who have discovered that there are clear clues to what makes a successful marriage. The Newport researchers have been conducting a study of married couples for the past ten years. They started with 50 pairs of newlyweds and interviewed them every six months. During that time, 11 of the couples dropped out of the study, 15 couples split up and 24 couples stayed married. The researchers were delighted that so many of their couples stayed together, but they don't think that it was simply a matter of luck.

One clear sign of a happy relationship is the frequent use of "we" by a couple. This is one indication that the couple speaks with a single voice about their experiences. Another clue is how past experiences are described. The happily married couples tend to focus on their experiences together, even when describing difficulties. As an example, two different couples described vacations in which their suitcases were lost. One couple (still married) reported that it was one of their best memories because they went out and bought some really different clothing and had a crazy time. Another couple (no longer married) ended up blaming each other for everything going wrong during the vacation.

Researchers have also noticed that individuals in successful marriages tend to talk about their spouses in much more positive ways. They focus on accomplishments. They often mention something new they enjoy doing now because of their partner. They also seem to be willing to change in ways that allow the couple to do things together. In marriages that aren't working, there is more focus on self. One of the individuals typically insists that he or she will not stop doing something despite the fact that it is a source of conflict. Sometimes one of them will say that he or she actually prefers it that the other has separate interests.

When the researchers asked couples what advice they would give to younger people thinking about getting married, they got some revealing answers. Among those who eventually got divorced, the man would often give a response that was quite different from the woman's. It was obvious that these individuals had really different views about marriage. Among those who remained married, the answers were more similar and often referred to the ideas of friendship, support, and "being on the same team." On the basis of their study, the researchers have concluded that a modern marriage may begin with passionate love, but its survival depends a lot on "companionate love," a feeling that includes affection, caring, and friendship.

B After reading the magazine article, decide whether these statements are true (T) or false (F).

1 In this article, the author claims that more than half of all marriages end in divorce. T / F
2 In the Newport study, more than twenty couples were interviewed twice a year for ten years. T / F
3 After ten years, the researchers found that three-quarters of the couples were still married. T / F
4 Couples who get divorced frequently speak with a single voice about their experiences. T / F
5 The researchers reported that happily married couples typically had separate interests. T / F
6 The researchers concluded that passionate love was the crucial factor in a long-term marriage. T / F

That-clauses

We can use noun clauses beginning with **that** (**that**-clauses) after verbs used to report thoughts (1) and feelings (2). We also use **that**-clauses to report statements in indirect speech (3).

    1 *People used to believe **that the earth was flat**. • I didn't realize **that you were waiting for me**.*
    2 *Do you ever feel **that you might be in danger**? • I always worry **that something could go wrong**.*
    3 *He mentioned **that he had seen the report**. • She whispered **that she would have to leave early**.*

We can also use **that**-clauses after nouns and adjectives.

    4 *I was faced with the problem **that I had no money**. • Were you surprised **that he passed the test**?*

In informal situations, we often use noun clauses without **that**, especially after the verbs **know**, **say**, and **think**.

    5 *I knew (that) **you'd finish first**. • Dan said (that) **he had a cold**. • Do you think (that) **it's OK**?*

We usually include **that** in formal uses (6), after nouns (7), and when a phrase (8) or a clause (9) comes between the verb and the **that**-clause.

    6 *A recent government study has concluded **that** drug use among adolescents is declining.*
    7 *A contract is a written agreement **that** you and/or others will do something.*
    8 *They discovered during the investigation **that** some money was missing.*
    9 *Sheila forgot when the meeting was and **that** she was supposed to unlock the door for us.*

We must include **that** (= "the fact that") when we use a **that**-clause as subject.

    10 ***That Juliet loved him** was never in doubt. • **That he said nothing** doesn't surprise me.*

Wh-clauses

We can use noun clauses beginning with **wh**-words such as **what**, **where**, and **how** (**wh**-clauses) after verbs used to report thoughts and questions (11). Like indirect questions, **wh**-clauses have the subject before the verb and no question mark (12).

    11 *I wonder **what it means**. • They don't know **where he went**. • He asked **how often we studied**.*
    12 *I can't understand **what she is saying**. (NOT ~~I can't understand what is she saying?~~)*

We can use **wh**-clauses, but not **that**-clauses, after prepositions.

    13 *He disagreed with **what we said**. • I read about **how he did it**. (NOT ~~I read about that he did it.~~)*

We can also begin noun clauses with **if** and **whether** after verbs used to report "not knowing" or an indirect yes/no question (14). We use **if/whether** when we are not sure (15) about the information expressed in the noun clause and **that** when we are sure (16).

    14 *I can't remember **if/whether I locked the door**. • He asked us **if/whether we were students**.*
    15 *Was he married? Genane didn't know. → Genane didn't know **if/whether** he was married.*
    16 *He was married. But Genane didn't know. → Genane didn't know **that** he was married.*

C Find examples of the following in the text on page 70

1 A **that**-clause reporting a statement: ....
2 A **that**-clause after a noun: ....
3 A **that**-clause after an adjective: ....
4 A **wh**-clause used to report a question: ....
5 A **wh**-clause after a preposition: ....

Noun clauses as subjects and objects

Noun clauses as subjects or after empty subject **it**

We can use a noun clause beginning with **that** (= "the fact that") (1) or a **wh**-word (2) as the subject before a verb, but usually only in formal situations.

1 *That we won the game* *surprised everyone.* • *That the other team played badly* *really helped us.*
2 *How the thieves broke in* *is obvious, but* *why they only took one old computer* *is a mystery.*

Instead of putting the noun clause in subject position, we usually use **it** as an empty subject and put the **that**-clause (3) or the **wh**-clause (4) at the end.

3 *It surprised everyone* *that we won the game.* • *It really helped us* *that the other team played badly.*
4 *It's obvious* *how the thieves broke in*, *but it's a mystery* *why they only took one old computer.*

We can use **whether** or **if** in a noun clause at the end after **it** as subject (5), but only **whether** in a noun clause in subject position (6).

5 *It doesn't really matter* *whether/if you go now or later.*
6 *Whether* *you go now or later doesn't really matter.* (NOT ~~If you go now or later doesn't matter.~~)

Noun clauses as objects or after empty object **it**

We can use a noun clause as an object after a verb to express facts (7) or ideas (8), and in indirect speech (9).

7 *We learned* *that pineapples don't grow on trees.* • *No one noticed* *that the keys were missing.*
8 *She could never anticipate* *what he might want.* • *Donald suggested* *that we should leave early.*
9 *He screamed* *that he hated school.* • *She said* *that she felt that everyone was against her.*

After verbs such as **show** and **tell**, we include an indirect object (**you, me**) before a noun clause as direct object.

10 *I'll show* ***you*** *how it works.* • *He told* ***me*** *that he loved me.* (NOT ~~He told that he loved me.~~)
Other verbs used like this include **assure, convince, inform, notify, persuade, remind, warn**

After verbs of "liking" (or "not liking"), we use **it** as an empty object before a noun clause.

11 *He doesn't* ***like it*** *that she still smokes.* • *I* ***hate it*** *that nobody ever cleans up after the meetings.*

After "thinking" verbs such as **consider** and **think**, we can use **it** as an empty object plus a noun (12) or adjective (13) before a noun clause. After verbs such as **regard, see,** or **view**, we use **it** + **as** before a noun or adjective and a noun clause (14).

12 *They consider* ***it an offence*** *when women go out in public without covering their heads.*
13 *We thought* ***it odd*** *that no one called us.* (NOT ~~We thought odd that no one called us.~~)
14 *Many people regard* ***it as a really bad idea*** *that Parliament approved the bill.*

A Find one example (from 7–14 above) for each category below.

1 "Feeling" verbs (**fear, sense, worry**): she felt that everyone was against her. (9)
2 "Learning" verbs (**discover, find, realize**): ....
3 "Noticing" verbs (**observe, perceive, recognize**): ....
4 "Predicting" verbs (**expect, forecast, hope**): ....
5 "Showing" verbs (**demonstrate, indicate, reveal**): ....
6 "Speaking" verbs (**explain, mention, whisper**): ....
7 "Suggesting" verbs (**advise, propose, recommend**): ....
8 "Thinking" verbs (**believe, conclude, imagine**): ....

B Rewrite these sentences in a less-formal style beginning with it.

1 That they don't have any money left doesn't surprise me at all.

....

2 That children would rather sit watching TV instead of playing outside just astonishes me.

....

3 Why the government didn't act immediately to stop the movement of all animals has never been explained.

....

4 Whether Nicole's father had been for or against her marriage wasn't clear, but he did participate in the wedding ceremony.

....

C Add one set of words to each paragraph (not necessarily in this order).

it / that / that   it / that / what   that / where / whether

A He wanted to know (1) .... we were doing, but (2) .... was obvious
  (3) .... he didn't really seem very interested in our answer.
B Sometimes one of them will say (4) .... he or she actually prefers
  (5) .... (6) .... the other has separate interests.
C (7) .... Mohammad's new plan will be an improvement remains to be seen, but
  no one liked it (8) .... he just decided (9) .... the changes would be
  made without consulting anyone.

D Correct the mistakes in these sentences.

1 Mr. Lafitte complained about the noise was predictable, but we assured it wouldn't happen again.

....
....

2 The principal warned during our meeting some teachers wouldn't like their classrooms had suddenly been changed.

....
....

3 They told me about Jeff had said in the meeting, but I thought strange he hadn't mentioned money.

....
....

4 The police regarded suspicious the dead woman's husband had recently taken out a life insurance policy in her name.

....
....

5 The prosecutor showed the jury how could the crime have been committed by Ms. Scott, but he didn't convince that Ms. Scott was guilty.

....
....

Nouns with noun clauses

Noun clauses after nouns

We often use noun clauses after nouns derived from those verbs listed in exercise A on page 72 (**conclude—conclusion, indicate—indication**). We usually include **that** after these nouns.

    1 *Her **conclusion that** boys are faster is wrong.*
    2 *There have been some recent **indications that** the economy is slowing down.*

Others include **belief, discovery, expectation, feeling, observation, proposal, realization**

We can also use noun clauses after nouns expressing possibility, often omitting **that** in informal situations (3). After nouns such as **issue** and **question**, we include **of** before a **wh**-clause (4).

    3 *There's a **possibility (that)** I'll be in town next week. Is there any **chance (that)** we can meet?*
    4 *We considered the **issue of what** we mean by freedom. • It's a **question of how** we can survive.*

Other nouns used with **of** include **consideration, discussion, example, knowledge, matter, problem, review**

Parenthetical noun clauses are sometimes used after nouns as a way of providing extra information or as a reminder. They are separated by commas (5), dashes (6), or parentheses (7).

    5 *His excuse**, that he had fallen asleep on the bus,** was hard to believe.*
    6 *One idea—**that Elvis is still alive**—keeps coming up in interviews with fans.*
    7 *They were questioning her about her first explanation **(that there had been a burglar)** when she suddenly changed her story completely.*

Noun clauses after nouns plus linking verbs (**be, seem, appear**)

We can use the verb **be** between a noun and the noun clause used to refer to it (8). In informal uses, we often leave out **that** after **be** (9).

    8 *One **theory is that** gravity travels at the speed of light. Our **concern is how** we can test the theory.*
    9 *Matt's basic **problem was (that)** he had failed two tests. The **truth is (that)** he never studies.*

We can use a noun plus **seem** or **appear** before **to be** and a noun clause (10). We can also use the empty subject **it** plus **seem** or **appear** (without **to be**) before a noun clause (11).

    10 *The assumption **seemed/appeared to be that** we would all pay more for high-speed service.*
    11 ***It seems that** it was too expensive. • **It appears that** they didn't do any real market research.*

The fact that …

We can use **the fact that** (rather than **that**) to introduce a noun clause as a subject or an object (12). After verbs such as **discuss**, we must use **the fact that** (not **that**) to introduce a noun clause (13).

    12 ***The fact that** he was married didn't bother her. She also ignored **the fact that** he had children.*
    13 *We discussed **the fact that** he had been absent a lot. (NOT ~~We discussed that he had been absent a lot.~~)*

Other verbs used like this include **conceal, dispute, disregard, hide, overlook, support**

We also use **the fact that** (not **that**) after prepositions (14) and phrasal verbs (15). We can use other nouns with more specific meanings such as **idea** or **news** instead of **fact** in these structures (16).

    14 *He pointed **to the fact that** the province is an island. (NOT ~~He pointed to that the province is an island.~~) • **Despite the fact that** she's small, she's very strong. (NOT ~~Despite that she's small, …~~)*
    15 *They **covered up the fact that** people had died. (NOT ~~They covered up that people had died.~~)*
    16 *I don't agree with **the idea that** older is wiser. • They played down **the news that** prices had increased.*

Noun clauses with **that** or relative clauses with **that**?

We can use the word **that** after a noun to introduce a noun clause (17) or a relative clause (18).

    17 *The story **that** he was in an accident isn't true. (NOT ~~The story which he was in an accident …~~)*
    18 *The story **that** he told us isn't true.*

A Rewrite these sentences as a single sentence using a noun derived from the verb in the sentence above it, plus other appropriate changes.

▶ I expected that the task would be simple. That was obviously too optimistic.
My <u>expectation that the task would be simple was obviously too optimistic.</u>

1 He explained that he had been stuck in traffic for over an hour. It didn't sound right.
His ....

2 They discovered the boy suffered from asthma. It changed their attitude.
Their ....

3 People believe there are aliens from outer space living among us. It's very widespread.
The ....

B Complete this report with these phrases plus *that* where necessary.

belief, example of, against the idea, to the fact, conclusion was, in agreement, despite the fact, with the view

In our group we discussed the death penalty. Two people agreed (1) .... the death penalty was necessary for serious crimes. They pointed (2) .... it was still used in many US states as punishment for murder and their (3) .... it acted as a deterrent, stopping people from committing crimes. One woman argued (4) .... the death penalty could stop or reduce crime. She said that the US provided an (5) .... what happens when a society is based on violence. (6) .... they had the death penalty, the US continued to have the worst crime rates and most-violent crimes. It was her (7) .... no government should be allowed to kill its own people, even if they are criminals. The others in our group were generally (8) .... there should not be a death penalty.

C Using a dictionary if necessary, complete the following definitions with these nouns plus *that*.

déjà vu, premonition, skepticism, superstition

1 A .... is a feeling .... something is going to happen, often something .... is unpleasant.

2 .... means having doubts .... statements are true or .... something will happen.

3 A .... is a belief .... events happen in a way .... cannot be explained by reason.

4 .... is the sense .... you have already experienced something .... is happening now.

D Correct the mistakes in the use of noun clauses in this text.

the idea that

According to one definition, the women's movement is a social and political movement promoting/ men and women should have equal rights in society. It tries to raise issues how equality can be accomplished by first getting people to recognize the fact which women don't have equal opportunity. It is based on the belief people's attitudes can be changed and the assumption other peaceful changes can be made through the legal system, in spite of it is largely controlled by men.

Relative clauses and relative pronouns

Relative clauses are usually introduced by relative pronouns such as **that, who,** or **which** and are used to provide information about someone or something just mentioned. We can use relative clauses to identify people (*I've just seen the woman **who lives upstairs***), describe things (*She's climbing up a ladder **that wobbles with every gust of wind***), and add comments (*I think she's going to clean her windows, **which seems dangerous in these circumstances***). We can sometimes use a relative clause with no relative pronoun (*With every step _ **she takes**, water splashes out of the bucket _ **she's carrying***).

A Read through this text and find one relative clause in each paragraph.

A The recent discovery of the wreck of an old ship on the ocean floor near the coast of North Carolina has revived interest in the colourful character who was the ship's last captain. The ship is believed to be the *Queen Anne's Revenge*, which sank in 1718. Her captain, who was the most notorious pirate of his day, was named Blackbeard.

B Blackbeard, whose real name was Edward Teach, had been a sailor on British ships in the Caribbean during Queen Anne's War (1702–1713). These ships were often involved in attacks on French and Spanish ships in the region and were allowed to keep a percentage of whatever they captured from these enemies of the queen.

C All this changed in 1713 when the European powers declared peace and the war ended. Teach and hundreds of other sailors had to choose between returning to unemployment in Britain or continuing to do what they knew best, only as pirates. They started as small bands in small boats, attacking and robbing merchant ships, and eventually took control of larger ships that had the speed and power to dominate the trade routes in and near the Caribbean. When they captured a large French ship, which they renamed *Queen Anne's Revenge*, Blackbeard and his crew finally had a true pirate ship, 80 feet long, with three masts and more than three dozen cannons.

D Blackbeard soon learned that a fearsome reputation, a pirate flag, and some warning shots from his cannons were all that he needed to stop most ships without a fight. In contemporary accounts, Blackbeard is described as a "demon from hell," whose huge black beard was twisted into long tails and who carried several guns and swords in belts slung across both shoulders. Sticking out from the sides of his cap were long smouldering fuses that he could use to ignite cannons during an attack.

E Blackbeard's reign of terror lasted until 1718 when he was killed in a sea battle with two British ships that had been sent to put an end to piracy in the region. After his death, Blackbeard became a romantic figure and stories about his daring adventures and tales of secret buried treasure helped to create the popular image of pirates we still have today. ■

B Complete this description using the appropriate relative pronoun or no relative pronoun (Ø).

Between 1713 and 1718, a pirate, (1)..................... real name was Edward Teach, but (2)..................... was known as Blackbeard, attacked ships (3)..................... sailed in and near the Caribbean. This pirate, (4)..................... some described as a "demon from hell," had a large black beard (5)..................... was twisted into long tails. He wore belts across both shoulders in (6)..................... he carried guns and swords. His pirate days came to an end in 1718 (7)..................... he was killed in a sea battle, but the stories (8)..................... spread about his adventures helped to create the romantic image of pirates (9)..................... we have today.

Relative clauses

We use a relative clause to give more information about a noun phrase in a preceding clause. Instead of repeating the subject noun phrase, we can use a relative pronoun (**who**, **that**).

1 I have a friend. <u>The friend</u> OR <u>He</u> lives in Antigonish. → *I have a friend **who lives in Antigonish**.*
2 We found a store. <u>The store</u> OR <u>It</u> sold old records. → *We found a store **that sold old records**.*

When we use a relative pronoun instead of an object noun or pronoun, we put the relative pronoun at the beginning of the relative clause. We don't repeat the noun or pronoun.

3 I loved the card. You sent <u>it</u>. → *I loved the card **that** you sent.* (NOT … ~~the card that you sent it.~~)
4 He's one man. I admire <u>him</u>. → *He's one man **whom** I admire.* (NOT … ~~whom I admire him.~~)

We usually try to put relative clauses immediately after the noun phrases they describe (5), but we can include a preposition phrase between the noun phrase and the relative clause (6).

5 The food came in plastic bags. We had to eat <u>the food</u>. → *The food **that we had to eat** came in plastic bags.* (NOT ~~The food came in plastic bags that we had to eat.~~)
6 *A pirate is <u>a person</u> on a ship **who** attacks and steals from other ships.*

Relative pronouns: **who, whom, which, that**

We use **who** and **whom** when we are referring to people. We can use **who** as the subject of a relative clause (7) and **whom** as the object (8). In casual speech, we sometimes use **who** as the object or, more commonly, leave out the relative pronoun (9).

7 Arvid is a teacher. <u>He</u> works in Calgary. → *Arvid is a teacher **who** works in Calgary.*
8 The person wasn't Arvid. You met <u>him</u>. → *The person **whom** you met wasn't Arvid.*
9 *The person **who** you met wasn't Arvid. / The person _ you met wasn't Arvid.*

We use **whom** after prepositions at the beginning of a relative clause. We can also put the preposition after the verb and use **whom** at the beginning or, more commonly, leave out the relative pronoun.

10 The man is Joe Nash. You should talk <u>to him</u>. → *The man **to whom** you should talk is Joe Nash. / The man **whom** you should talk **to** is Joe Nash. / The man   you should talk **to** is Joe Nash.*

We use **that** for things or animals (11) and after group nouns such as **team** for a group of people we are thinking of as a single unit (12).

11 *I found the keys **that** were missing. • They own a cat **that** doesn't have a tail.*
12 We were on the team. <u>The team</u> won the cup. → *We were on the team **that** won the cup.*

We can use **which** after prepositions at the beginning of a relative clause in formal situations. In informal situations, we put the preposition after the verb and use **that** at the beginning of the relative clause or, more commonly, we leave out the relative pronoun.

13 I can't remember the hotel. We stayed <u>in the hotel</u>. → *I can't remember the hotel **in which** we stayed. / I can't remember the hotel **(that)** we stayed **in**.* (NOT … ~~the hotel we stayed in it.~~)

C In the text on page 76, find two relative clauses beginning with *that* which could be used with no relative pronoun.

....

Defining and non-defining relative clauses

Defining relative clauses

In a defining relative clause, we include information that identifies or classifies people (1) and things (2). The meaning of the sentence is not complete without the defining relative clause.

1 *Do you remember the woman **who used to work in the bookstore**? She's a teacher now.*
2 *Do you have a thing **that measures temperature**? ~ You mean a thermometer? Sorry, I don't.*

We often use (**that**) at the beginning of a defining relative clause instead of the object (3) or the object of a preposition (4). We usually use (**that**) after noun phrases containing superlatives (5) or quantifiers (6).

3 I brought the dictionary. Maria wanted <u>it</u>. → *I brought the dictionary **(that)** Maria wanted.*
4 The movie is *Water*. He's talking <u>about it</u>. → *The movie **(that)** he's talking **about** is* Water.
5 *It's the **best** movie **(that)** I've seen in years. • It was the **worst** class **(that)** I had at school.*
6 *There's **a lot (that)** I don't know about computers. • **Every** dog **(that)** we saw wore a sweater.*

We can also begin defining relative clauses with **who** and **whom**.

7 *I don't know anyone **whom** I can trust. • The man **who** plays trumpet in the band was onstage.*

Non-defining relative clauses

When we want to include essential information, we use a defining relative clause (8). When we are simply adding extra information, we use a non-defining relative clause (9). We usually put a comma before a non-defining clause and a comma after it, unless it is the end of the sentence.

8 *The first caller **who can give the correct answer** will win the prize.*
9 *The first caller, **who was from the Surrey area,** didn't give the correct answer.*

We can also use parentheses or dashes: *The second caller **(who sounded older)** got it right.*

We usually use **who**, **whom**, or **which** at the beginning of non-defining relative clauses (10). We don't usually begin non-defining relative clauses with **that** or without a relative pronoun (11).

10 *Our new boss, **who seems to be nice,** has said nothing about Mr. Downing, **whom he replaced.***
11 *The Mini, **which some people initially laughed at,** soon became the most popular car.*
   (NOT *The Mini, (that) some people initially laughed at, soon became the most popular car.*)

We can use non-defining relative clauses with **which** to add comments about preceding statements (12). We also use **which** in preposition phrases such as **in which case** at the beginning of non-defining relative clauses used to add comments (13).

12 *They said Catherine had been in prison, **which simply wasn't true.***
13 *There may be a strike, **in which case** the office will remain closed.*

In non-defining relative clauses we can use **of which** and **of whom** after quantifiers such as **some** (14) or superlatives such as **the most famous** (15). We do this when we want to add information about part of something or about an individual from a group already mentioned.

14 *The last lecture, **some of which** I just didn't understand, was about osmosis.*
15 *At the conference, there were several writers, **the most famous of whom** was Yann Martel.*

We can also put superlatives after the relative pronoun: *… writers, of whom the most famous was …*

A In the text on page 76, find two relative clauses beginning with *which*. Are they defining or non-defining?

....
....

B Add one set of relative pronouns (not necessarily in this order) to each description.

that / which / who (×2) / whom   that (×2) / which / who (×2)

Greenpeace is an organization (1) .... was started by a group of activists
(2) .... wanted to make a difference. In 1971, the founding members got in their
fishing boat, (3) .... was named *Greenpeace*, and sailed toward the island of
Amchitka, where they hoped to prevent the detonation of a nuclear bomb. They were concerned
the explosion would cause earthquakes and tsunamis (4) .... could harm humans,
animals, and the environment. The group didn't make it to the island, but their actions inspired others
(5) .... protested further explosions on Amchitka.

A "Jekyll and Hyde" is a person (6) .... has two personalities, one of
(7) .... is bad and the other good. The expression comes from a novel about Dr. Jekyll,
(8) .... investigates the good and evil parts of human nature and invents a drug
(9) .... can separate them. When he takes the drug, he becomes an evil version of
himself, (10) .... he calls Mr. Hyde.

C Add one of these clauses to each of the sentences below. Use relative pronouns and
make other appropriate changes. Add commas where necessary.

he or she controls a sporting event   most people know him as Mark Twain
some of them are poisonous   it uses exaggerated actions, often involving accidents
it consists of nine islands   the largest part of it is below the surface of the water
you rent a room or apartment from him   each competitor takes part in three different sports in it
~~he has never been married~~

▶ A bachelor is a man who has never been married.
1 Slapstick is a type of comedy ....
2 A referee is an official ....
3 A triathlon is an athletic event ....
4 A landlord is a person ....
5 An iceberg .... is a solid
mass of ice floating in the ocean.
6 Snakes .... are long reptiles without legs.
7 Tuvalu .... is a country in the South Pacific.
8 Samuel Clemens .... was a major American writer.

D Correct the mistakes in the use of relative clauses in this text.

                that
A strange thing/happened to me once was getting a letter said I had been "terminated." The letter,

that came from the university, was an official notice of termination (means "the end") of

employment. It was like being fired from my job, which it felt really weird. I didn't have a job at the

university that I could be fired from it! I was just a student didn't have a job. When I called the office,

they said it was an error had been caused by a new computer. I wasn't the only one had been

terminated by that computer. A lot of other people didn't have jobs at the university lost them that day.

Conditionals; zero and first conditionals (real conditionals)

Conditional sentences present one event, typically in a clause beginning with **if** (*If I don't leave the house before 7:30*), as a condition for another event, expressed in a main clause (*I usually miss the bus to work*). In real conditionals, the events happen, have happened, or are likely to happen (*If I miss the bus, I have to walk all the way to work*). In unreal conditionals, the events have not happened, are not likely to happen, or are imaginary (*If I lived near work, I wouldn't have this problem*).

A Read through these paragraphs and find two *if*-clauses with verbs in the Simple Past

1 another expressing a real condition
2 one expressing an unreal condition

Anna

She started when she was fourteen. She wanted to be just like the boys. In those days, if she had a cigarette in her hand, she was cool. That's what they all thought back then. But it's easier to start than to stop. She is trying to quit, but it isn't simple. If she has a cup of coffee, she always wants to smoke a cigarette.

Raina

She had always known that she wasn't the fastest or the most talented. Her mother had once told her, "If you are successful, it will be because of hard work." And that was how she had approached her tennis. Like going to work. She saw the other kids just hanging around while she ran to tennis practice. She had spent her whole life on tennis courts. Now she had won her first championship. She heard her mother's words, "If you don't experience a struggle, you won't experience the triumph."

Mai-Lei

The teacher was describing a movie about a farmer who had turned one of his fields into a baseball park. The farmer had heard a voice telling him, "If you build it, he will come." She wanted us to write about that as our topic. I couldn't imagine that happening where I live. I like swimming, but if I put a huge swimming pool in front of my house, people would think I was crazy. Plus, I wouldn't want people coming to my pool. If I went to all that trouble, I would put the pool at the back of my house.

Jamal

"If I were you, I would sell it." That was his sister's advice in response to his request for help. She was putting on her coat and getting ready to leave. If he had wanted to sell his car, he would have done that already. But he didn't have a job, so he couldn't really afford to keep the car. It was his own fault, he knew that. If he had worked harder at school, he would have had some kind of career by now. That obviously wasn't happening. "If you were in my situation, I would help you out!" he called out to his sister.

Erin

When she was younger, she didn't care about anything. She thought she was really tough. If she caught a cold, she didn't stop. Nothing could get her down or make her stay at home. But these days she gets sick really easily, so she has to pay more attention. If she catches a cold, she goes to bed immediately. She doesn't try to be tough because she's not as strong as she used to be.

B Choose one of the following as the final sentence of each paragraph (Anna–Erin).

1 And I would build a high fence around it. (......................)
2 But she isn't complaining. (......................)
3 She has had to avoid one so that she can avoid the other. (......................)
4 But she had already left. (......................)
5 Now she knew what they meant. (......................)

Zero conditional

We use a zero conditional (or factual conditional) to express a fixed connection that exists between two events now or always (**if** + present tense + present tense).

    1 *If I **wash** the dishes, he **dries** them. • If the fruit **feels** soft, it's ready to eat.*

We can also use zero conditionals to express a connection that existed before now (**if** + past tense + past tense).

    2 *If it **rained**, we **took** the bus. • If my uncle **caught** fish, he always **gave** us some.*
Note that it is only in zero conditionals that **if** is used with a meaning similar to "when."

First conditional

We use a first conditional (or predictive conditional) to express a likely connection between one event (**if** + present tense) and another possible event (**will**).

    3 *If your friends **don't arrive** by five, we'll **leave** without them. • If I **see** Eva, I'll **tell** her.*

The most common modal used in the main clause is **will**, but we also use other modals and phrasal modals such as **can** and **be going to**.

    4 *If we **get** there early, we **can** sit at the front. • If he **says** that again, I'm **going to** scream!*

We don't usually put **will** in the **if**-clause unless it is part of a polite invitation or request (5).

    5 *If you'll just follow me, I'll take you to your room. • If you'll open the door, I'll bring these in.*

C Find an example of each of the following in the paragraphs on page 80.

1 a present tense zero conditional

....

2 a past tense zero conditional

....

3 a first conditional

....

D Choose an ending (a–f) for each beginning (1–6). Choose the correct verb.

1 If there <u>is/was</u> a lot to do, (...)   a she won't do well.
2 If the students <u>come/came</u> to us, (...)   b we can't make you do it.
3 If the test <u>is/will be</u> difficult, (...)   c she takes the bus.
4 If there <u>is/was</u> a lot to carry, (...)   d we can usually help them.
5 If you <u>don't/didn't</u> want to study, (...)   e we ask the porter to help us.
6 If it <u>is/was</u> cold and wet, (...)   f everyone helped.

Second and third conditionals (unreal conditionals)

Second conditional

We use a second conditional (or hypothetical conditional) to express a distant and unlikely connection between one imaginary event (**if** + past tense) and another imaginary event (**would**).
   1 *If I **got** the job, I'd move to Halifax.* • *If you **lived** closer, we'd visit you more often.*
The past subjunctive (**were**) is also used in a second conditional: *If I were you, I'd go.*

The most common modal in the main clause is **would**, but we also use other modals such as **could** and **might**.
   2 *If you **came** in the summer, you **could stay** with us and you **might** even **get** your own room.*

We don't usually put **would** in the **if**-clause unless we are using it to express a desired outcome.
   3 *If he **would** only behave himself, I'd take him with me.* • *If it **would** stop raining, we'd go.*

Third conditional

We use a third conditional (or counterfactual conditional) to express an imaginary connection between one event that never happened (**if** + Past Perfect) and another event that also never happened (**would have** + past participle).
   4 He didn't call me. I didn't help him. → *If he **had called** me, I **would have helped** him.*

The most common modal in the main clause is **would have**, but we also use other modals such as **might have** and **could have**.
   5 *If she **had asked** us, we **might have known** how to fix it, or we **could have tried** at least.*

The contracted form **you'd** can be **you had** in the **if**-clause or **you would** in the main clause.
   6 *If you**'d seen** him, you**'d have laughed**.* (= If you **had** seen him, you **would** have laughed) •
   *We**'d have been** really disappointed if they**'d lost**.* (= We **would** have … if they **had**)

A **Find an example of each of the following in the paragraphs on page 80.**

   1 a second conditional

   ....

   2 a third conditional

   ....

B **Complete each sentence with an unreal conditional using information from the sentences above it.**

   ▶ I don't have extra pens. I won't give you one.
      If *I had extra pens, I would give you one.*
   1 I don't know Jason's phone number. I can't tell him what happened.
      If ....
   2 She didn't study for the test. She didn't pass.
      If ....
   3 You didn't warn us about the bad weather. I didn't bring a toque and mitts.
      If ....
   4 I'm not in your situation. I'll start looking for another job.
      If ....

C Choose one of these verbs for each blank in the text.

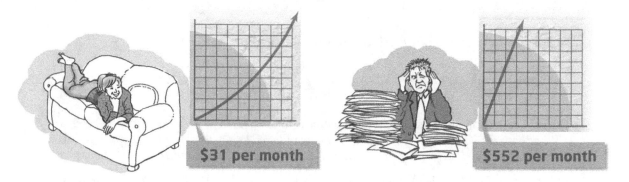

$31 per month

$552 per month

decided, were, would contribute, would start, started, had started, would cost, would have contributed, wanted, could do, would end up, could have paid

How many times have you heard, "If I (1) .... you, I (2) .... saving now for retirement"? If you (3) .... to have $100,000 at age 65, you (4) .... it for as little as $31 per month. The earlier you start, the lower your monthly payments will be and the lower your total payment (the amount you contribute) will be.

Look at Sandra. She's 24 now. Beginning next year, if she (5) .... investing $31 every month, she (6) .... only $14,880 in total over forty years. So, she'd invest less than $15,000 in total and receive $100,000 from her investment.

Now look at David. He's 55. If he (7) .... investing at 30, he (8) .... only $46 every month and (9) .... $19,320. But if he (10) .... to start investing now, it (11) .... $552 every month and he (12) .... paying a total of $66,240. Doesn't it make sense to start early?

D Correct the mistakes in the use of conditionals in this text.

My mother keeps trying to give me a big old armchair that used to belong to my grandparents. I remember that, when I was a child, if my grandpa ~~sit~~ ^sat^ in that chair after dinner, he always fall asleep. He snored too. If his feet are near the fire, his slippers start to smoke and my grandma has to rush over and wake him up. I have also noticed recently that if my father sit in that chair, he immediately go to sleep and start snoring. My mother get really annoyed if that happen. It's like a chair with a curse. I am worried that if I take the chair, the same thing happen to me. I don't have this dilemma if my older brother didn't move away two years ago. If he stays, he is given the chair first and I am not faced with the problem. But it is a really nice-looking chair and maybe I could make room for it. If I move a small table, the chair fit in my living room next to the fire. Do I really have a problem if I settle into its comfortable embrace after dinner and give in to its seductive charms? But who wake me up if my slippers catch fire?

The uses of conditionals

A Write the numbers of the appropriate examples in the spaces.

Zero conditionals: **What happens if … ? What happened if … ?**

We use zero conditionals to describe typical patterns in the present ⬚ or the past ⬚.
1 *What happens if there's a lot of demand? If demand increases, prices usually go up.*
2 *What happened if there was bad weather? If it was really bad, crops failed and people starved.*

We can use zero conditionals to express rules ⬚, habits ⬚, and correlations, such as scientific observations ⬚. We can also use them with imperative forms in the main clause when we are explaining how to do something ⬚.
3 *If people earn more, they spend more. • If the paper turns red, the solution is acid.*
4 *If it was a nice Sunday afternoon, we always went for a long walk.*
5 *If the ball touches the line, it's in, not out.*
6 *If you need customer service, press 1. If you want to place an order, press 2.*

First conditionals: **What will happen if … ?**

We use first conditionals to describe possibilities.
7 *What will happen if the situation gets worse? ~ If things get worse, we'll leave the country.*

We can use first conditionals for plans ⬚ and predictions ⬚. We can also use them with questions in the main clause to ask about future events ⬚ or to make requests ⬚.
8 *If we have time later, we'll go to the theatre and get tickets for the concert.*
9 *If Montreal's quarterback is healthy, they'll win easily.*
10 *If you have a moment, will you check this for me?*
11 *If the camps are closed, where will these people go?*

Second conditionals: **What would happen if … ?**

We use second conditionals to describe imaginary or fictional situations.
12 *What would happen if a volcano erupted underneath the ocean? ~ If a volcano erupted underneath the ocean, there would be a huge tidal wave.*

We can use second conditionals to refer to completely imaginary situations ⬚, or to describe the potential outcomes of a course of action ⬚. We can also use them when we want to express willingness to do something, despite lack of ability ⬚.
13 *If I were feeling better, I would help you move your boxes.*
14 *If Canada were a dictatorship, there wouldn't be democratic elections.*
15 *If they agreed to make classes smaller, we could give each student more attention.*

Third conditionals: **What would have happened if … ?**

We use third conditionals to imagine past events happening in a different way and having different outcomes.
16 *What would have happened if she hadn't said "Yes"? ~ If she had said "No," I would have been devastated.*

We can use third conditionals when we express regret ⬚ or assign blame ⬚.
17 *If I had told her that I loved her more often, she might not have left me.*
18 *If you had listened to his advice, we wouldn't have lost all our money.*

B Each of these questions can be answered by one of the example sentences (1–18) on page 84. Decide which type of conditional each answer will be and choose the most appropriate sentence.

▶ Can you remember your childhood? What happened if the weather was nice
  (.zero., 4..............)

1 What do you think will happen if there's a Winnipeg–Montreal final? (.......................)
2 What happens in the economy if real wages rise? (.......................)
3 What would happen if your ideas about class size were adopted? (.......................)
4 Can you remember what the rule is if the ball hits the line? (.......................)
5 What would you have felt if Helen had given a negative answer? (.......................)
6 What do I do if I want to order something? (.......................)
7 What did he actually say would happen if he didn't have the flu? (.......................)
8 What would have happened if I had paid better attention to what our financial advisor said?
  (.......................)

C Choose an ending (a–e) for each beginning (1–5) and add these verbs:

don't want, had asked, hadn't forgotten, need, were

1 If you .... for directions, (...)
2 If this .... your car, (...)
3 If I .... to order the book yet, (...)
4 If we .... the bread, (...)
5 If you .... to talk to the operator, (...)

a would you lend it to other people?
b lunch would have been much better.
c we wouldn't have gotten lost.
d press 3.
e can I just examine one copy?

D Write each of these *if*-clauses on the appropriate blank.

if not, if you tried as hard as you could, if it's complete, if you've done your best, if that's your goal, if the only measure of success were becoming a doctor

I think I could have applied that approach to anything I might have chosen to do. It's no different from the person whose ultimate goal is to become a doctor.
    (1) .... and you're getting Cs in biology then the first thing you have to do is get Bs in biology and then As. You have to perfect the first step and then move on to chemistry or physics.
    Take those small steps. Otherwise you're opening yourself up to all kinds of frustration. Where would your confidence come from (2) ....?
(3) .... and didn't become a doctor, would that mean your whole life was a failure? Of course not.
    All those steps are like pieces of a puzzle. They all come together to form a picture.
(4) ...., then you've reached your goal.
(5) ...., don't get down on yourself.
(6) ...., then you will have had some accomplishments along the way.

Adverbial clauses and conjunctions

Adverbial clauses usually begin with conjunctions such as **although**, **because**, or **when**. The conjunction shows the relationship between the adverbial clause and the rest of the sentence. (***Although the sun's shining**, it's freezing outside this morning. I'm not going out **because it's so cold**.*)

We can use an adverbial clause (*I might go out **when it gets warmer***) to provide additional information about an action or situation in a way that is similar to an adverb (*I might go out **later***) or prepositional phrase (*I might go out **in the afternoon***).

A Read through the following text and find one adverbial clause in each paragraph.

A   After her husband passed away, Monique Lafleur continued to take care of the special garden he had created in front of their small house. She imagined that Henri was "up there" and looking down from time to time, so she tried to take good care of his proud creation.

B   Before he began his career with the national weather service, Henri had studied geography and art. Although he'd had to give up his artistic ambitions, Henri still managed to find ways to be creative in his spare time. He had designed and created something unique in their garden.

C   It wasn't a garden in the usual sense. There were no plants. Monique had tried to put in some flowers around the edges, but they always died. Her neighbour, Ms. Perez, said it was probably because there was all that cement in the soil. Henri hadn't known, when he was mixing the cement, sand, and water, then pouring it out into the wooden frame, that his concrete map would end up as the only thing in the garden, apart from the weeds that grew in small cracks in the river valleys.

D   When there was a period of warm summer weather, the weeds would spread out from the cracks, especially in the Prairies around the Winnipeg area. Before Monique could get to them, they would almost be in Iqaluit, a wild patch of green in the pale grey expanse of the rest of the country.

E   The busiest time was autumn, when Monique had to go out and sweep the whole country every morning. If it wasn't wet, she could just use a brush to push the leaves down through the Maritimes and sweep them away in the general direction of the Atlantic. When it rained a lot, she would stand inside, watching the leaves pile up in a soggy mess over most of British Columbia.

F   Even though it wasn't really cold during most of the winter, there would occasionally be freezing days of snow and sleet, after which Henri's concrete map would be transformed into a shining sculpture of pure ice. The rough edges of Canada would change into smooth glistening lines and the country would become an abstract shape, as if it had been carved from a large flat slab of marble by an expert hand. On a cold clear December morning, Monique would look out at the sculpture in her garden with a strong sense that, at that very moment, Henri was also looking down and enjoying the scene. He had used weather to create art from geography.

B After reading the text above, decide whether these statements are true (T) or false (F).

1 Henri Lafleur had studied art before he worked for the national weather service. T / F
2 When Henri died, his wife created a concrete map of Canada in their garden. T / F
3 While he was mixing the concrete, Henri decided that his map would be the only thing in the garden. T / F
4 Weeds grew in the cracks because the flowers Monique planted always died. T / F
5 If the weather was dry, Monique could brush the leaves off the map. T / F
6 When the weather was freezing in winter, the map looked like an ice sculpture. T / F

Adverbial clauses

We can use an adverbial clause (**before he left**) as part of a sentence in a way that is similar to an adverb (**earlier**) or a prepositional phrase (**at ten o'clock**).

1 *I talked to Francisco **before he left**.* = *I talked to Francisco **earlier**.* = *I talked to Francisco **at ten o'clock**.*

We usually put an adverbial clause after the main clause in the sentence (2). If we put an adverbial clause before the main clause, we include a comma between the two (3).

2 *You won't pass the test **if you don't study**.* • *We had to turn on the heat **because it was cold**.*

3 ***If you don't study**, you won't pass the test.* • ***Because it was cold**, we had to turn on the heat.*

We sometimes use more than one adverbial clause in a sentence.

4 *Don't touch the paint **before it has dried** + **because bubbles may form** + **if anything touches it**.*

Conjunctions

We use a subordinating conjunction such as **after** or **while** to connect an adverbial clause to another clause and to show how the meanings of the two clauses are related.

5 ***After you take a break**, you'll probably feel better.* • *I can't listen to music **while I'm studying**.*

Other subordinating conjunctions include **as, as if, as soon as, if, in order to, since, so, so that**

When we connect an adverbial clause to another clause, we use a single conjunction (6). We don't use an adverbial clause as a separate sentence (7).

6 ***Because there were no lights**, I couldn't see anything. It was dark **so I couldn't do any work**.* (NOT ~~Because there were no lights, so I couldn't do any work.~~)

7 *We couldn't use our computers **because there was no electricity this morning**.* (NOT ~~We couldn't use our computers. Because there was no electricity this morning.~~)

We can use some words, such as **after, before**, and **than**, as conjunctions with adverbial clauses or as prepositions with noun phrases (8). After conjunctions, we use subject pronouns (**we, they**) plus verbs (9). After prepositions, we use object pronouns (**us, them**) (10).

8 *I'll talk to you **after I get out of my next meeting**.* = *I'll talk to you **after the meeting**.*

9 *Tony had arrived **before we got there**.* • *We had more money **than they had**.*

10 *Tony had arrived **before us**.* • *We had more money **than them**.*

Some conjunctions that we use with adverbial clauses (**because, although, while**) have similar meanings to prepositions used with noun phrases (**because of, despite, during**).

11 *There were delays **because** the weather was bad.* = *There were delays **because of** bad weather.*

12 ***Although** she's over 70, Fran still plays tennis.* = ***Despite** her age, Fran still plays tennis.*

13 *He got injured **while** we were playing.* = *He got injured **during** the game.*

C In the text on page 86, find adverbial clauses with meanings similar to these phrases.

1 After her husband's death: ....

2 Because of the cement: ....

3 During warm summer weather: ....

4 Despite the usually mild winter weather: ....

5 Like a carving: ....

Time clauses

When, while, as

We can use **when** at the beginning of an adverbial clause describing a period of time (1) or a point in time (2).
  1 *When I was young, we didn't watch TV.* • *Most people don't have cars **when they're students.***
  2 *When we heard the news, we were delighted.* • *I'll check my email **when I get to work.***
Note that we don't use **will** in the **when**-clause. (NOT ~~I'll check my email when I will get to work.~~)

We also use clauses beginning with **when** to describe something that happens soon after something else in another clause (3) or that interrupts something in another clause (4). We can use **when** like **if** in a zero conditional to refer to "every time" something happens (5).
  3 *We had just reached the shelter **when the rain started pouring down.***
  4 *I was sleeping like a baby **when the alarm went off.***
  5 ***When demand increases,*** *prices rise.* • *The roof used to leak **when we had heavy rain.***

We can use a clause with **while** ("during the period that") or **when** to describe a period of time with another clause to describe what happens at some point in that period of time (6). We often use **while** to connect clauses in which two things happen at the same time for the whole period of time (7).
  6 ***While / When you were out,*** *your mother called.* • *I fell asleep **while/when I was reading.***
  7 *There was nowhere to park, so I just drove around in the car **while Kevin was in the bank.***

We can use **as** like **when** and **while** for a period of time during which something happens (8). We can use **as** or **just as** (not **while**) to focus on the precise moment that something happens (9). We also use **as** to show a connection between one type of change over time and another (10).
  8 ***As / When / While I was getting ready to leave,*** *I heard that my flight had been cancelled.*
  9 ***As I walked out of the hotel,*** *a gust of wind blew my hat off. It happened **just as I stepped outside.***
  10 ***As I get older,*** *I care less about what other people think.* (NOT ~~While I get older, I care less~~ …)

A Complete each sentence in such a way that it is as similar as possible in meaning to the sentence above it.

  1 I watched Maurice drive by in his new car while I was standing at the bus stop in the rain.
    When ....

  2 You'll know that the fruit is getting ripe when the skin starts to turn yellow.
    As ....

  3 We shouldn't talk about anything to do with work during lunch.
    While ....

  4 I was getting out of the shower when the phone rang in the other room.
    Just as ....

B Using information from the text on page 86, draw a circle around the appropriate conjunction(s) in the following sentences. More than one conjunction may be appropriate.

  1 When / While Henri started working for the national weather service, he'd given up his artistic ambitions.
  2 When / While it was wet during the autumn months, Monique couldn't brush the leaves away.
  3 As / While the weather got warmer, weeds would spread out from the cracks.
  4 As / When / While Monique looked at the sculpture on a cold clear December morning, she had a sense that Henri was doing the same thing.

After, before, until, since, etc.

We use **after** ("at a point later than") in an adverbial clause when the other clause describes something that happens later (11). We use **before** ("at a point earlier than") in the adverbial clause when the other clause describes something that happens at any time earlier (12). We often use **after** with the Simple Present or Present Perfect (not **will**) for a completed action (13).

 11 ***After they left,*** *we cleaned up and went to bed.* • *What will you do **after you graduate**?*
 12 ***Before he leaves,*** *I'll ask him about the money. They had eaten breakfast **before we got up**.*
 13 *I'll help you **after I write / have written my report**.* (NOT ~~after I will write my report~~)

We use **until** ("up to the time that") to focus on the end point or outcome of something (14). We use **since** ("from the time that") to describe a starting point for something in another clause that happens later or that is still true (15).

 14 *We'll wait **until you're ready**.* • *Heat the wax **until it melts**.* (NOT ~~Heat it before it melts.~~)
 15 *How long is it **since you've been there**?* • *I've lived here **since I was ten**.* (NOT ~~after I was ten~~)
We use the Present Perfect or Simple Past (not Simple Present) after **since** (NOT ~~since I'm ten~~).

We can use **once** to introduce a clause that describes a starting point for another action or situation. We often use **once** like **after** with the Simple Present or Present Perfect in a clause describing something as completed.

 16 ***Once you've seen Ani,*** *you won't forget her.* • *Everyone likes it here **once they get used to it**.*

When we want to explain that one thing happens very quickly after another, we can use **as soon as** and **immediately** to introduce the clause with the first action (17). Phrases such as **the instant / minute / moment / second** (**that**) are used in the same way (18).

 17 *I came **as soon as I heard the news**.* • ***Immediately after I saw him,*** *I recognized his face.*
 18 *There are some students who rush out of the room **the minute (that) class ends**.*

C Using a dictionary if necessary, complete these descriptions with the following words.

blender, postscript, prediction, skewer, after, before, until, while

1 A .... is a statement about an event .... it happens.
2 A .... is a wooden or metal stick pushed through pieces of meat or vegetables to hold them .... they are cooking.
3 A .... is extra information added .... a letter or story is complete.
4 A .... is a machine for chopping or mixing pieces of food .... they become a liquid.

D Complete these sentences with *have ('ve) been* or *will ('ll) be*.

1 Where will the refugees go after the camps .... closed?
2 I'm sorry about the delay, but I .... back as soon as I have checked this.
3 My back still hurts and it will soon be two weeks since I .... at work.
4 I'm sure we .... in Peterborough in August, so we can visit your new house then.
5 The moment we hear that the airport is open, relief supplies .... loaded on to the waiting aircraft.
6 New students should not register for classes until they .... given their student numbers.
7 Once you .... here for a few weeks, you won't want to leave.
8 The children .... hungry when they come back from swimming this morning.

Manner and reason clauses

Manner clauses

We can use manner clauses beginning with **as** ("in the form or way that") (1) and **just as** ("in exactly the form or way that") (2) when we are describing how something was or how something was done.

    1 *The movie depicts life **as it was in 1900**. • Complete each exercise **as I showed you.***

    2 *I wrote the note **just as you told me to**. • Everything happened **just as my mother had predicted**.*

We use **as if** and **as though** with the same meaning in manner clauses after verbs such as **look, seem, sound, taste,** etc. (3). We can also use **as if / though** after verbs such as **act, behave,** and **talk** when we are describing behaviour (4).

    3 *Can I help you? You look **as if you're lost**. • He sounds **as though he might be getting a cold**.*

    4 *She always tries to act **as if she's my boss**. • They talked about it **as though it was worthless**.*

The subjunctive **were** is sometimes used after **as if / though**: *He treats me as if I were a child.*

In informal situations, **like** is sometimes used instead of **as** or **as if.**

    5 *No one will ever love you **like I do**. • It feels **like winter has suddenly arrived**.*

Note that **like** is often used as a preposition: *It feels like winter.* (NOT ~~It feels as winter.~~)

We use **as … as** ("in the same way that") to say that two actions or situations are similar or different in some way (6). Between the first and second **as** we can put adjectives and adverbs (7) or quantifiers such as **many** and **much** (8).

    6 *Is Max still funny in the same way that he used to be?* → *Is Max still **as funny as he used to be**?*

    7 *The weather isn't **as hot as** it was last year. • We didn't play **as well as** we did against Vancouver.*

    8 *Were there **as many** problems **as** you anticipated? • It didn't cost **as much as** he said.*

We sometimes form the negative with **not so … as**: *Ben is not so naïve as you think.*

A **Choose the best answer (a–d) for each question (1–4) and add *as* or *as if*.**

    1 Did she seem afraid? (…)   a No, she was just ………… you had described her.

    2 Had she changed much? (…)   b Yes, she did it ………… she was supposed to.

    3 Did she fit in well? (…)   c Yes, she looked ………… she had seen a ghost.

    4 Did she write it correctly? (…) d Not really, because she acted ………… she was better than us.

B **Add one of these clauses, introduced by *as though*, *just as*, or *as … as*, to the following sentences. Make any other necessary changes.**

~~everyone has been saying~~, it really is, the guidebook had described it, I remembered it, it was made yesterday, they have done, nothing had happened

▶ Is the new Italian restaurant ^as good ….. as everyone has been saying ……?

    1 No one talked about it. They all behaved ………………………………………………

    2 I went to see my old school and it hadn't changed. It was still …………………………

    ………………………

    3 This coffee is terrible. It tastes …………………………………………………

    4 When you emulate someone successful, you try to do well, ………………………………

    5 We found the little cottage hidden in the forest, ………………………………………

    6 If you underestimate the cost of something, you think it isn't much, …………………

    ………………………

Reason clauses

We use **because** at the beginning of a clause to give a reason or explanation for something (9) or to support a statement in an earlier clause (10).

9 ***Because there had been an accident,*** *we all arrived late.* • *I didn't eat* ***because I wasn't hungry.***

10 *He says he didn't drive through a red light, but I know he's lying,* ***because I saw him do it.***

We sometimes use **as** or **since** instead of **because** in reason clauses (11). We can use **as** or **while** to refer to time and reason together ("while and because") (12). We can use **since** to refer to a starting point and a reason together ("from that time and because") (13).

11 ***As it was late,*** *we decided to stop working.* • ***Since she knew Latin,*** *I asked her to translate it.*

12 ***As / While we're on the subject of money,*** *I'd like to ask about next year's budget.*

13 ***Since his wife left him,*** *he's been depressed.* • ***Since it's been snowing,*** *we've stayed indoors.*

We can use **now (that)** like **since** ("from that time and because") to introduce a clause explaining a present situation. We usually use the Simple Present or Present Perfect after **now (that)**.

14 ***Now (that) we're married,*** *we never go out.* • *I enjoy opera* ***now (that) I've learned more about it.***

In formal situations, other conjunctions such as **for** (15) and **in that** (16) are sometimes used instead of **because** to add a reason or explanation for a preceding statement.

15 *It would be wise to save some of the money,* ***for there may be unexpected expenses later.***

16 *We definitely have a problem* ***in that there are more students than we have room for.***

C **Complete each sentence in such a way that it is as similar as possible in meaning to the pair of sentences above it.**

1 All the banks will be closed on Monday. It's a holiday.
   As ....

2 She has had to use crutches. She had an operation on her foot.
   Since ....

3 We're all together today. We should decide on a date for the barbecue.
   While ....

4 I wonder what he'll do next. He has finished his exams.
   Now that ....

D **Match a sentence from the first group (1–4) with one from the second group (a–d) that has a similar meaning. Add *as if* or *because*.**

▶ I'd love to go out more, but I haven't had much free time lately. (e)

1 It's more expensive to eat in a restaurant, but I don't like to cook. (...)

2 If I wanted to avoid doing something, I pretended to be sick. (...)

3 The price of beef is higher now, but I don't eat any, so my food budget hasn't increased. (...)

4 No matter what the discussion is about, no one ever pays attention to my suggestions. (...)

a .... I'm a vegetarian, I'm spending less than other people these days.

b I acted .... I wasn't feeling well when I didn't want to do things.

c I spend more money on meals .... I don't make them myself at home.

d They always treat me .... I have nothing useful to say.

e I haven't been to a movie or a play in ages ..... because ..... I've been busy at work.

Connectors and focus structures

Connectors are words such as **consequently, however,** and **so** and phrases such as **in addition, in fact,** and **for example** that are used to link clauses and sentences. (*The Japanese economy has been very strong and **consequently** the yen has risen in value. **In addition**, the dollar has continued to show weakness. The pound, **however**, has remained steady.*)

Focus structures are also used to link sentences. One type of focus structure is called fronting. In fronting, one part of a sentence (*I can't eat asparagus*) is moved to front position in order to focus attention on that part. (*I can eat broccoli and carrots. **Asparagus** I can't eat.*)

Another type of focus structure is a cleft sentence. In a cleft sentence, we focus attention on one part of a sentence and put the other part of the sentence in a separate clause. We can begin a cleft sentence with **it** (***It's** asparagus I can't eat*) or **what** (*What I can't eat is **asparagus***).

A Read through this text and find one connector in each paragraph.

A All those people who say that the weather hasn't been normal recently are right. However, since there is really no such thing as normal weather, they probably mean
5 something else. If they mean that average summer temperatures have been getting warmer, then they are certainly correct. In fact, it is not just the summer temperature, but the general average temperature of the whole
10 world that has been steadily moving up.
B The signs are everywhere. There are small signs. For example, butterflies in North America have moved about 100 kilometres north of where they used to live. There are
15 also very large signs. Huge masses of ice in mountain glaciers and the Arctic are melting. The famous snow cap on Africa's Mount Kilimanjaro has almost disappeared. Actually, ice or snow doesn't really disappear, it turns
20 into water, flows into the ocean and causes sea levels to rise.
C Why is this happening? One answer is that it could simply be part of a natural process. After all, there have been long periods of
25 warmth in the past. So we could just be experiencing another warming trend. This kind of answer had more supporters a few years ago. What scientists now believe is that human activity is the cause. For more than two
30 hundred years, humans have been gradually changing the atmosphere, mainly as a result of industrial pollution. We have created an atmosphere around the earth that, like a giant glass container, lets heat from the sun through
35 and holds it inside.
D Will temperatures and sea levels keep rising? Should we just move to higher ground and throw away our winter coats? The answer depends on where you live. If you live on the
40 coast of Florida, the answer is a definite yes. However, if you live in Canada, your winter temperatures may soon be on the way down. The warmer temperatures and increased fresh water cause heavier winter snowfall in the
45 Arctic. As a consequence, Arctic air currents are changing and cold polar air is beginning to drift south. According to one prediction, winter in Canada, and in much of the Northern Hemisphere, could be getting
50 more severe.

B Choose one of the following as the final sentence of each of the paragraphs (A–D) above.

1 It may be a good idea to hold on to your winter coat. (…)
2 It's known as the greenhouse effect. (…)
3 It's called climate change. (…)
4 As a result, small islands in the Pacific are going under. (…)

Adverbs as connectors

The most common connectors are adverbs such as **however** or **then** that we can use to link a sentence (1) or clause (2) to a preceding sentence or clause. They are also called linking words.

    1 *We wanted to rent an apartment near the university.* **However,** *they were all too expensive.*
    2 *The elderly woman poured two cups of tea,* **then** *I asked her if she remembered my grandparents.*
Others include **actually, also, finally, instead, later, meanwhile, secondly, so, therefore**

We usually put adverbs used as connectors at the front of the sentence or clause (3). The only connectors we don't use in front position are **as well** and **too**. We can use them and other connectors in end position (4). We can also use connectors in mid position, after **be** or auxiliary verbs (5) and before the main verb (6). Not all connectors can be used in all possible positions.

    3 *I've been to Morocco several times.* **Actually,** *I've just come back from there.*
    4 *I spent a few days in Casablanca. I visited Rabat and Tangier* **as well.**
    5 *Don't forget your raincoat. You are* **also** *going to need an umbrella.*
    6 *Dave and Aki arrived with steaming hot coffee. They* **also** *brought fresh rolls.*
We don't usually put a connector between a verb and its object. (NOT ~~They brought also fresh rolls.~~)

Phrases as connectors

We use some prepositional phrases as connectors, usually in front position (7), but sometimes in mid (8) or end position (9). Not all prepositional phrases used as connectors can be put in all possible positions. We usually separate phrases used as connectors with commas.

    7 *The doctor will see you soon.* **In the meantime,** *could you please fill out these forms?*
    8 *We have your application, but it's incomplete. You didn't,* **for example,** *include a photograph.*
    9 *One man lied about having a degree in English. He had never been to university,* **in fact.**
Others include **as a result, for a start, in addition, in conclusion, in other words, on the other hand**

We can also use infinitive phrases such as **to begin with** as connectors, usually in front position.

    10 *I had a summer job on a farm, but I didn't enjoy it.* **To begin with,** *I had to start at six, which meant I was always tired.*
Others include **to conclude, to start with, to summarize, to sum up**

Focus structures

We can use focus structures to link sentences. We can move one part of a sentence to front position to link that sentence more closely to the preceding sentence. This is called fronting.

    11 I'd rather visit Montreal than Vancouver these days. (I don't like Vancouver as much as I used to.)
    → <u>*Vancouver*</u> *I don't like as much as I used to.*

We can also use focus structures to emphasize one part of a sentence, usually when we are making a contrast with, or adding to, information in a preceding sentence. Sentences like this, which begin with **it** (12) or **what** (13), are called cleft sentences.

    12 I didn't eat the strawberries. (Jackie ate them.) → *It was <u>Jackie</u> who ate them.*
    13 We didn't like the way he spoke. (We really didn't like his rude behaviour.) → **What** *we really didn't like was <u>his rude behaviour</u>.*

C **Find examples of the following in the text on page 92:**

  1 a sentence with a connector in mid position: ....
  2 a focus structure beginning with **what**: ....

Connectors, prepositions, and conjunctions

Connectors or prepositions?

Some connectors (**as a result, in addition**) are similar to complex prepositions (**as a result of, in addition to**). Instead of a connector (1), we sometimes use a complex preposition plus a noun phrase (2) or a pronoun (3) at the beginning of a sentence.

    1 *As a result, sea levels are rising. **In addition**, they discussed the situation in the Pacific.*

    2 ***As a result of these changes,** sea levels are rising.* (NOT *As a result of sea levels are rising.*)

    3 ***In addition to that**, they discussed the situation in the Pacific.* (NOT *In addition that, …*)

Other complex prepositions include **as an example of, in comparison to / with, in contrast to**

We can also use a complex preposition plus a noun phrase or pronoun (4), or a similar connector (5), in end position.

    4 *Malcolm went to Dalhousie. Sarah chose McGill **instead of Dalhousie**.*

    5 *He went to Dalhousie. She chose McGill **instead**.* (NOT *… McGill instead Dalhousie.*)

Connectors or conjunctions?

We can use connectors such as **also** and **however** in a way that is similar to the coordinating conjunctions **and** and **but**. We use the connectors when we want to emphasize the type of connection, such as adding (6) or contrasting (7).

    6 *Angelique's doing great these days. She's living in the country. She **also** has a new boyfriend. • She's living in the country **and** she has a new boyfriend.*

    7 *I sometimes drink coffee in a restaurant. **However**, I prefer tea most of the time. • I sometimes drink coffee in a restaurant, **but** I prefer tea most of the time.*

We sometimes use coordinating conjunctions before connectors in the same clause when we want to emphasize the type of relationship, such as result (8) or contrast (9), between the clauses.

    8 *She didn't sign the contract **and consequently** it isn't legal.* (NOT *consequently and*)

    9 *They were trapped for two days, **but nevertheless** they survived.* (NOT *nevertheless but*)

We sometimes reduce clauses after coordinating conjunctions, but not after connectors.

    10 *The show was supposed to start early, **but** didn't.* (NOT *… however didn't.*)

Although connectors and conjunctions can both link clauses inside sentences, we usually use conjunctions to join clauses within the same sentence (11) and connectors to link sentences (12).

    11 *You can stay here **and** help me **or** you can go inside, **but** you can't just sit watching TV.*

    12 *We were working outside all day. **Meanwhile**, he was sitting inside watching TV.*

We can use **so** and **though** as connectors or as subordinating conjunctions. When used as conjunctions, **so** and **though** introduce an adverbial clause as part of a sentence (13). When used as connectors, they link one sentence to another (14).

    13 *It was an interesting offer, **though** I couldn't accept it, **so** I said nothing.*

    14 *I'm sure it was her car outside. **So** she must have been at home. • We really liked their new apartment. It was gorgeous. It was very expensive, **though**.*

A **Using information from the text on page 92, complete these sentences with connectors, prepositions or conjunctions.**

    1 .... industrial pollution, the atmosphere has gradually changed.

    2 .... small changes such as butterflies moving north, there are large changes such as glaciers melting .... flowing into the ocean. Sea levels are rising ....

B Choose one phrase from each pair to complete these sentences from a history text.

in addition   in contrast   for example   as a result
in addition to   in contrast to   as an example of   as a result of

The Battle of the Plains of Abraham was fought between the British and the French on September 13, 1759 in what is now Quebec City. The two armies were about the same size, but the British troops were all regular soldiers; (1) .... , much of the French army was made up of poorly trained militia. It is not surprising that the British won the battle and (2) .... New France soon fell. Many people consider this one of the most important battles in the Seven Years' War. (3) .... affecting Canadian history, this battle had worldwide consequences. It is argued that the American Revolution, (4) .... , would not have occurred if France had not lost its North American territory to the British.

C Complete the description with these words:

also, and, as a result, but, however, so

The Titanic was considered to be the fastest and most modern passenger ship of its day. It was (1) .... believed to be unsinkable. During its first voyage in 1912, (2) .... , the ship hit an iceberg (3) .... sank. While the ship was slowly sinking, there was time for the passengers to escape, (4) .... there were not enough lifeboats, (5) .... hundreds of people drowned in the disaster. (6) .... , tough new laws were introduced to make ships much safer.

D Choose a sentence or clause (a–d) to follow each sentence or clause (1–4) and add these words:

and, but, instead, or, so (×2), though

1 We loved playing in the snow. (...)
2 I liked the car .... my wife loved it. (...)
3 I didn't think the test was long
  .... difficult, (...)
4 There wasn't a flight available. (...)

a .... some of the students did.
b .... we took the train
  ....
c .... we bought it.
d It was really cold, ...

E Correct the mistakes in the use of connectors in this text.

My friend Kazuko sometimes helps me with my English writing. She was born in Japan, ~~however,~~ but she spent part of her childhood in America consequently her English is really good. She isn't like an American, although. Americans seem to be very direct, in contrast this Kazuko is very indirect. As example, she never tells me that I have made a mistake. Instead that, she points to a line and takes a deep breath. She makes also a small "tsss" sound. Alternatively, or she may say some part needs "special attention." For her, nothing is ever wrong; it is simply "not finished yet." As a result this, I have not only learned English from her, but I have also learned how to be helpful and patient. Nevertheless that, I think that she will have to take a few deep breaths when she reads this. In other word, it is not finished yet.

Review test

There are four blanks in each of the following paragraphs.

Choose the best answer (**a**, **b**, **c**, **d**) for each blank. The correct answers are on pages 125–26.

1   After police arrested a man for breaking into a grocery store, they discovered that the thief was actually a teenage girl dressed as a man. Although they informed (1) _____ she didn't have to (2) _____ them anything, the girl confessed (3) _____ she had done it (4) _____ her family because they had no money and they were hungry.

1 a) her that	b) that	c) that her	d) to her that
2 a) admit	b) explain	c) report	d) tell
3 a) that	b) that to them	c) them that	d) them to that
4 a) by	b) for	c) that	d) to

2   Because it (1) _____ a lot recently, I (2) _____ out as much and I suspect you will have been (3) _____ why I haven't been in touch. I'm sorry about the long silence, but I (4) _____ to call you this week and maybe we can arrange to meet for lunch on Friday or Saturday.

1 a) has been raining	b) is raining	c) rain	d) rains
2 a) am not going	b) don't go	c) haven't gone	d) never go
3 a) believing	b) knowing	c) realizing	d) wondering
4 a) am promising	b) have been promising	c) have promised	d) promise

3   My grandfather said that when he (1) _____ up, he lived on a farm. During the summer, he (2) _____ to get up early every morning and work all day on the farm. He said that most people (3) _____ to go away on vacation, as they do now. But he (4) _____ feeling unhappy or deprived or anything like that because all of his friends were in the same situation.

1 a) had been growing	b) had grown	c) was growing	d) was grown
2 a) had been	b) has	c) was having	d) would have
3 a) didn't use	b) haven't used	c) wasn't used	d) weren't used
4 a) didn't remember	b) hadn't been remembering	c) hadn't remembered	d) wasn't remembering

4 The best summer vacation I (1) _____ was when I was ten and I went to stay
with my grandparents for a few weeks. At that time they were living in the country and
(2) _____ still go for long walks through the woods. I (3) _____ to climb trees
and run around with their dog. I (4) _____ go near the lake by myself, but
my grandfather sometimes took me fishing there.

1 a) am remembering	b) can remember	c) must remember	d) was remembering
2 a) can	b) could	c) may	d) might
3 a) could	b) could be	c) could have	d) was able
4 a) can't	b) may not	c) might not	d) wasn't allowed to

5 The Comfy Canuck hotel chain is in financial trouble and some of their smaller hotels are
closing, it (1) _____. Rising costs (2) _____ for recent losses and many smaller
hotels (3) _____ to have been losing money for many years. No buyer has yet
(4) _____ for the properties.

1 a) has been reported	b) is reporting	c) reports	d) been reported
2 a) are being blamed	b) blamed	c) have blamed	d) to be blamed
3 a) are reported	b) are reporting	c) been reported	d) have reported
4 a) been found	b) being found	c) found	d) to be found

6 (1) _____ poem we read in class today was "The Waste Land." It is (2) _____
poem by T.S. Eliot, first published in 1922. (3) _____ style of the poem has had a great
influence on (4) _____ modern poetry.

1 a) A	b) An	c) The	d) Ø
2 a) a	b) an	c) the	d) Ø
3 a) a	b) an	c) the	d) Ø
4 a) a	b) an	c) the	d) Ø

7 "I don't call this (1) _____ progress," says Josiah Neice, owner of (2) _____
small downtown business. He complains that an hour and fifteen minutes (3) _____
become his typical commuting time every morning. "It used to take only twenty minutes.
There's just too much (4) _____ now."

1 a) a	b) one	c) the	d) Ø
2 a) a	b) an	c) the	d) Ø
3 a) are	b) has	c) have	d) is
4 a) car	b) cars	c) vehicle	d) traffic

8 I'm really enjoying my new job. All of (1) _____ people I work with are friendly and I haven't had (2) _____ problems so far. The best part is that I get paid (3) _____ two weeks instead of waiting (4) _____ month between paycheques like in my last job.

1 a) that   b) the   c) them   d) Ø
2 a) any   b) much   c) some   d) no
3 a) all   b) both   c) each   d) every
4 a) a whole   b) the whole of   c) whole   d) whole of

9 I remember when we stayed (1) _____ Toronto (2) _____ a few days (3) _____ last summer. It was really hot, even (4) _____ night, and I just felt miserable.

1 a) at   b) in   c) into   d) Ø
2 a) by   b) during   c) for   d) in
3 a) at   b) on   c) in   d) Ø
4 a) at   b) by   c) during   d) in

10 When we were students, my friends and I rented a cabin (1) _____ the mountains so that we could go hiking. It only cost us $100 for the whole week, not (2) _____ food, of course. One day, my friend Daniel got tired and stopped to rest, saying he'd catch up with us (3) _____ an hour, but when he still hadn't returned to the cabin (4) _____ late afternoon, we started getting worried. Luckily, he met some men who were hunting in the area and they brought him back to the cabin before it got dark.

1 a) above   b) in   c) on   d) over
2 a) include   b) included   c) includes   d) including
3 a) for   b) in   c) by   d) at
4 a) by   b) during   c) in   d) since

11 When I visit big cities like Paris, I usually avoid (1) _____ to the most popular places because I really hate crowds. But it was no use (2) _____ that to my friend Tatjana because she really enjoys (3) _____ museums. We went to the Louvre and she refused (4) _____ outside while she went in.

1 a) go   b) going   c) gone   d) to go
2 a) trying explain   b) trying to explain   c) to try explaining   d) to try to explain
3 a) visits   b) to visit   c) visiting   d) visited
4 a) letting me to wait   b) letting me wait   c) to let me to wait   d) to let me wait

12 Andrew Reeb, former managing director of Delco Electronics, has pled "Not Guilty" to charges (1) _____ $5 million from the company. He claims not to know where (2) _____. He has suggested that an accountant (3) _____ the money. Investigators consider (4) _____ anyone else in the company could have committed the crime.

1 a) stealing   b) that he stole   c) to have stolen   d) which he stole
2 a) did go the money   b) did the money go   c) the money went   d) went the money
3 a) is taking   b) should take   c) takes   d) took
4 a) it unlikely that   b) that it unlikely   c) that unlikely   d) unlikely that

13 I've been looking for a special kind of brown cheese (1) _____ made in Norway, but I can't remember its name, (2) _____ is frustrating. There was one woman I talked (3) _____ in the Gourmet Experience shop on King Street (4) _____ said they could order it for me if I could give her more information about it.

1 a) it   b) that's   c) was   d) which
2 a) what   b) which   c) where   d) whose
3 a) to   b) to her   c) to whom   d) Ø
4 a) what   b) who   c) whom   d) Ø

14 Although their hair wasn't actually very long, rock groups such as the Beatles and the Rolling Stones were often criticized as "long-haired" or "needing haircuts." (1) _____ people didn't like the way these groups looked, they usually (2) _____ the groups' music as well. In the sixties men were considered effeminate if they (3) _____ long hair. The opposite was true for men who grew beards (4) _____, of course, the beards were allowed to grow too long.

1 a) Then   b) If   c) So   d) Only if
2 a) dislike   b) disliked   c) was disliking   d) have disliked
3 a) had   b) have   c) will have   d) would have
4 a) if   b) if not   c) only if   d) unless

15 I know you're anxiously waiting to find out if I passed my exams, but I haven't heard anything yet. Perhaps I'll get the news today when the mail (1) _____. I promise I (2) _____ you as soon as I get the news. It's been three weeks (3) _____ I took the exams, but my teachers warned me that they sometimes don't announce the results until more than a month (4) _____.

1 a) comes   b) came   c) is coming   d) will come
2 a) call   b) called   c) 'll call   d) 'm calling
3 a) later   b) once   c) since   d) when
4 a) has passed   b) is passing   c) passed   d) will pass

16 (1) _____ our flight from Halifax to Toronto was delayed because (2) _____ bad weather, we missed our connection to Vancouver. We read lots of magazines (3) _____ the six hours we spent at the airport. (4) _____ the delay, we still had a good trip and didn't feel too jet-lagged when we arrived.

1 a) After   b) Although   c) If   d) So that
2 a) it   b) of   c) the   d) Ø
3 a) before   b) although   c) during   d) while
4 a) Although   b) As   c) Despite   d) Unless

Appendix: Regular and irregular verbs

Regular verbs

We add **-ed** (1) or simply **-d** (2) to the base form of regular verbs to make the Simple Past and past participle forms.

1 *I ask**ed** him, but he hasn't answer**ed** yet.* • *We want**ed** to know.* • *I have wait**ed** patiently.*

2 *They agre**ed** that it was a good idea.* • *That's why we have continu**ed**.* • *She hasn't smil**ed** much.*

Before adding **-ed** to some verbs, we double the final consonant (after a single written vowel, in stressed syllables).

3 *She had pla**nn**ed to visit us and regre**tt**ed that poor health had sto**pp**ed her.*

Others include **dragged, occurred, permitted, preferred, ripped, robbed, slipped, trimmed**

We change the final **-y** (after a consonant) to **-i-** before **-ed** in some verbs.

4 *Have you tr**ied** to get a scholarship?* ~ *I appl**ied** for one, but they haven't repl**ied** yet.*

Others include **carried, copied, cried, hurried, identified, implied, studied, testified, worried**

Irregular verbs

We use special forms for the Simple Past of some verbs.

5 *We **saw** Riyaad Ali yesterday.* • *I **forgot** I had your keys.* • *They **understood** what I **taught** them.*

We add **-en** (6) or **-n** (7) to the base form of some verbs to make the past participle.

6 *Where have you be**en**?* • *Have you eat**en** anything?* • *I had hidd**en** it, but it had fall**en** out.*

7 *I haven't se**en** that movie.* • *Have you know**n** him a long time?* • *They've drive**n** up from Moose Jaw.*

We use the base form of some verbs for the Simple Past and past participle.

8 *Yesterday I **hit** my forehead on the shelf and **cut** it, but it hasn't **hurt** too badly today.*

Others include **bet, burst, cost, forecast, let, put, quit, ride, set, shut, split, spread, thrust**

Some verbs are used with both regular and irregular forms.

9 *Who <u>burned</u> / burnt the toast?* • *I dreamed / <u>dreamt</u> about you.* • *He <u>spilled</u> / spilt some milk.*

Others include **kneeled / <u>knelt</u>, leaped / <u>leapt</u>, <u>learned</u> / learnt, lighted / <u>lit</u>, speeded / <u>sped</u>**

Note that the underlined form of each verb is currently more common in Canadian English.

Common irregular verbs

BASIC FORM	SIMPLE PAST	PAST PARTICIPLE
be	was, were	been
become	became	become
begin	began	begun
bend	bent	bent
bet	bet	bet
bite	bit	bitten
blow	blew	blown
break	broke	broken
bring	brought	brought
build	built	built
burst	burst	burst
buy	bought	bought
catch	caught	caught
choose	chose	chosen
come	came	came
cost	cost	cost
cut	cut	cut
dig	dug	dug
do	did	done
draw	drew	drawn
drink	drank	drunk
drive	drove	driven
eat	ate	eaten
fall	fell	fallen
feed	fed	fed
feel	felt	felt
fight	fought	fought
find	found	found
fly	flew	flown
forget	forgot	forgotten
forgive	forgave	forgiven
freeze	froze	frozen
get	got	got
give	gave	given
go	went	gone
grow	grew	grown
have	had	had
hear	heard	heard
hide	hid	hidden
hit	hit	hit
hold	held	held
keep	kept	kept
kneel	knelt	knelt
know	knew	known
lay	laid	laid
lead	led	led
leave	left	left
lend	lent	lent
let	let	let
lie	lay	lain

BASIC FORM	SIMPLE PAST	PAST PARTICIPLE
light	lit	lit
lose	lost	lost
make	made	made
mean	meant	meant
meet	met	met
pay	paid	paid
put	put	put
read	read	read
ride	rode	ridden
ring	rang	rung
rise	rose	risen
run	ran	run
say	said	said
see	saw	seen
sell	sold	sold
send	sent	sent
set	set	set
shake	shook	shaken
shine	shone	shone
shoot	shot	shot
show	showed	shown
shut	shut	shut
sing	sang	sung
sink	sank	sunk
sit	sat	sat
sleep	slept	slept
slide	slid	slid
speak	spoke	spoken
spend	spent	spent
spit	spat	spat
split	split	split
spread	spread	spread
stand	stood	stood
steal	stole	stolen
stick	stuck	stuck
strike	struck	struck
swear	swore	sworn
sweep	swept	swept
swim	swam	swum
take	took	taken
teach	taught	taught
tear	tore	torn
tell	told	told
think	thought	thought
throw	threw	thrown
understand	understood	understood
wake	woke	woken
wear	wore	worn
win	won	won
write	wrote	written

Glossary

This is a list of grammar terms with explanations of what they mean. Words printed in CAPITALS in the explanations are themselves grammar terms and can be found in their own place in the glossary.

action verb: a VERB used to describe what we do or what happens (*I **ate** lunch.*); compare STATIVE VERB

active verb: a VERB form used to describe what the SUBJECT does (*A thief **stole** my car.*); compare PASSIVE

adjective: a word such as **new** or **good-looking** used to modify a NOUN (*Katia's **new** boyfriend is **good-looking**.*)

adverb: a word such as **really** or **recently** used to modify a VERB, ADJECTIVE, ADVERB, or SENTENCE (*I met him **recently** and he's **really** good-looking.*)

adverbial: an ADVERB (**later**), PREPOSITIONAL PHRASE (**in town**), or ADVERBIAL CLAUSE (**after I finish work**) used to provide additional information in a CLAUSE or a sentence (*I'll meet you **in town** **later** **after I've finished work**.*)

adverbial clause: a CLAUSE typically introduced by a SUBORDINATING CONJUNCTION such as **because** and providing information such as when or why something happens (*I can't go out **because I have to study**.*)

agent: the person or thing that does or causes an action, typically the SUBJECT in ACTIVE sentences (***Patrick deWitt** wrote The Sisters Brothers.*)

article: a word used as a DETERMINER before a NOUN, either as a DEFINITE ARTICLE (**the**) or an INDEFINITE ARTICLE (**a/an**) (***The** car had **a** flat tire.*)

attributive adjective: an ADJECTIVE used before a NOUN (*She had **red** hair and **green** eyes.*); compare PREDICATIVE ADJECTIVE

auxiliary verb: a form of **be, do, have,** or a MODAL used with a MAIN VERB to form different TENSES, negatives, and QUESTIONS (***Have** you eaten yet?*)

bare infinitive = base form

base form: the form of a VERB such as **be** or **eat**, as listed in a dictionary

clause: a group of words including a SUBJECT and a VERB that forms a SIMPLE SENTENCE (*She left yesterday.*) or is part of a COMPLEX SENTENCE (*She left before you came.*) or COMPOUND SENTENCE (*She left and I'm glad.*)

cleft sentence: a structure in which a sentence (*I'm not supposed to drink coffee.*) is divided into two parts and attention is focused on one part, using an IT-CLEFT (*It's coffee that I'm not supposed to drink.*) or a WH-CLEFT (*What I'm not supposed to drink is coffee.*)

collective noun = group noun

common noun: a NOUN that is not the name of anyone or anything (*The **car** had a flat **tire**.*); compare PROPER NOUN

comparative: an ADJECTIVE or ADVERB with **-er** (**healthier**) or **more/less** (**less expensive**), often followed by **than**, used to say that something has more or less of a quality than another (*Fish is **healthier** and **less expensive** than meat.*); compare SUPERLATIVE

complement: a word or phrase used after a LINKING VERB, typically describing the SUBJECT (*She is **a student** so she isn't **rich**.*)

complex preposition: a PREPOSITION that consists of two or more words (*In addition to me, there were three other people waiting in front of the entrance.*); compare SIMPLE PREPOSITION

complex sentence: a sentence with two or more CLAUSES joined by a SUBORDINATING CONJUNCTION such as **because, before,** etc. (*I went to bed because I was tired.*); compare COMPOUND SENTENCE

compound adjective: an ADJECTIVE that consists of two words joined by a hyphen (*a good-looking person, a home-cooked meal*)

compound-complex sentence: a sentence with three or more CLAUSES joined by both a COORDINATING CONJUNCTION and a SUBORDINATING CONJUNCTION (*Dave read a magazine and I went to bed because I was tired.*); compare COMPLEX SENTENCE and COMPOUND SENTENCE

compound noun: two or more words used together as a NOUN to refer to a person or thing (*a bus driver, an application form*)

compound sentence: a sentence with two or more CLAUSES joined by a COORDINATING CONJUNCTION (**and, but,** or **or**) (*Dave read a magazine and I went to bed.*); compare COMPLEX SENTENCE

conditional: a structure in which one CLAUSE, typically beginning with **if,** is presented as a condition for something in another clause (*If I have time, I'll help you.*)

conjunction: a word such as **and, but,** or **or** that links words, phrases, or sentences (*It's late and I want to go home.*)

connector: a word (**however**) or phrase (**in addition**) typically used to link sentences and sometimes CLAUSES (*They didn't win. **However,** they played better than they did last week. **In addition,** they scored two goals.*)

continuous = progressive

contracted form: a short form of a word (**I've, he's, she'd, we'll, they won't**)

coordinating conjunction: and, but, or (*I'll write or I'll call you.*); compare SUBORDINATING CONJUNCTION

countable noun: a NOUN that can be singular (**book, child**) or plural (**books, children**) and used to refer to people or things as separate individuals; compare UNCOUNTABLE NOUN

counterfactual conditional = third conditional

defining relative clause: a RELATIVE CLAUSE used to identify or classify people or things (*Do you know the man **who lives upstairs?***); compare NON-DEFINING RELATIVE CLAUSE

definite article: the (*Can you see the moon?*); compare INDEFINITE ARTICLE

demonstrative: one of the words **this, that, these,** or **those** used as a DETERMINER before a NOUN (***this** book*) or as a PRONOUN instead of a NOUN PHRASE (*I don't like **that.***)

demonstrative pronoun: one of the words **this, that, these,** or **those** used instead of a NOUN PHRASE (*I like **these** better than **those.***)

determiner: a word used before a NOUN such as an ARTICLE (**a/an, the**), a DEMONSTRATIVE (**this, that, these, those**), or a POSSESSIVE (**my, your, his, her, its, our, their**) (*A friend sent me **this** funny card for **my** birthday.*)

direct object: a word or phrase identifying the one(s) affected by the action of the verb (*I dropped **the ball.***); compare INDIRECT OBJECT

direct speech: the original words of a speaker, usually presented in QUOTATION MARKS, in a report of what was said (*He said, "**I'm tired.**"*); compare INDIRECT SPEECH

ellipsis: the practice of leaving out words or phrases instead of repeating them (*Raj came in and __ sat down.*)

empty object *it*: the word **it** in DIRECT OBJECT position, not used to refer to anything (*I hate **it** when I miss the bus.*)

empty subject *it*: the word **it** in SUBJECT position, not used to refer to anything (***It** was nice to go for a walk even though **it** was raining.*)

empty subject *there*: the word **there** in SUBJECT position, not used to refer to anything (***There** isn't any food left.*)

equative: an ADJECTIVE or ADVERB in the structure (**not**) **as ... as**, used to describe something as similar (or not) to another in some way (*Your cat is **as** big **as** my dog.*)

factual conditional = zero conditional

first conditional: a type of REAL CONDITIONAL used to express a fixed connection between two events now, in the past, or always (*If the fruit is soft, it's ready to eat.*)

focus structure: a structure such as FRONTING or a CLEFT SENTENCE used to focus attention on one part of a sentence (***Tea** I can drink. It's **coffee** I'm not supposed to drink.*)

fraction: a word or phrase such as **half** or **two-thirds** used as a QUANTIFIER with **of** before a DETERMINER or PRONOUN to describe a part of something (***Two-thirds of** the students are from Japan.*)

fronting: a structure in which one part of a sentence (*I can't drink coffee*) is moved to front position (***Coffee** I can't drink because it gives me a headache.*)

generic noun: a NOUN used in making a general statement about something, not about a specific example (***Women** live longer than **men.***)

generic pronoun: a PRONOUN such as **one, they, we,** or **you** used with the meaning "people in general" (***They** say **you** can't teach an old dog new tricks.*)

gerund: a word with the same form as the PRESENT PARTICIPLE, but used as a NOUN (*I enjoy **walking.***)

group noun: a NOUN such as **committee** or **team** used to refer to a group of people as a single unit (*The **committee** chooses the national **team.***)

hypothetical conditional = second conditional

imperative: the BASE FORM of the VERB, typically used to give orders (***Stop!***)

indefinite adverb: an ADVERB such as **anywhere** or **everywhere** used to describe places in a very general way (*I've looked **everywhere,** but I can't find my notebook **anywhere.***)

indefinite article: **a** / **an** (*Would you like **an** apple or **a** banana?*); compare DEFINITE ARTICLE

indefinite pronoun: a PRONOUN such as **someone** or **anything** used to describe people and things in a very general way (***Someone** called earlier, but he or she didn't say **anything.***)

indirect object: a word or phrase used after a VERB such as **give** or **send,** identifying the person or thing receiving something (*I gave **Bob** some money. I sent a letter to **them.***); compare DIRECT OBJECT

indirect question: a version of a previously asked QUESTION, not the exact words, presented in a NOUN CLAUSE as a report of a WH-QUESTION (*He asked **what we were doing**.*) or a YES/NO QUESTION (*He asked **if we were from Sweden**.*)

indirect speech: a version of a previous utterance, not the exact words, presented in a NOUN CLAUSE as a report of what was said (*He said **that he was tired**.*); compare DIRECT SPEECH

infinitive: to plus the BASE FORM of a VERB (*I'm hoping **to win**.*)

-ing form = gerund

intransitive verb: a VERB that never has an OBJECT (*I can't **sleep**.*); compare TRANSITIVE VERB

inversion: a structure in which a VERB or AUXILIARY VERB is put before the SUBJECT (*Into the room **walked two men**.*)

it-cleft: a structure in which a sentence (*I'm not supposed to drink coffee.*) is divided into two parts, the first part with **it** + **be** + an emphasized element and the second part a RELATIVE CLAUSE (*It's coffee (that) I'm not supposed to drink.*); compare WH-CLEFT

linking verb: a VERB such as **be**, **become**, or **seem**, used with a complement, typically describing the SUBJECT (*She **is/seems** unhappy.*)

linking word = connector

main verb: the VERB in a CLAUSE (*Did you **follow** that? I **understood** what she said.*); compare AUXILIARY VERB

mass noun = uncountable noun

mixed conditional: a type of CONDITIONAL in which there is an unusual combination of TENSES in the two CLAUSES (*If you saw the movie, you'll remember the battle scene.*)

modal: an AUXILIARY VERB such as **can**, **could**, or **must**, used with the BASE FORM of a VERB to describe what is possible, permitted, necessary, etc. (*You **must** leave now.*); compare PHRASAL MODAL

multiplier: a word or phrase such as **twice** or **five times** used as a QUANTIFIER before a DETERMINER to describe how often or how much more something is (*They pray **five times** a day.*)

negative: a sentence or CLAUSE with an AUXILIARY VERB plus **not** or **-n't** and a MAIN VERB (*I **don't** care.*)

negative adverb: a word or phrase such as **never** or **no longer** used as an ADVERB (*He **never** studies.*)

nominal clause = noun clause

non-count noun = uncountable noun

non-defining relative clause: a RELATIVE CLAUSE used to provide extra information, typically set off by commas (*My friend Pedro, **who lives upstairs**, has a cat.*); compare DEFINING RELATIVE CLAUSE

non-finite form = base form

noun: a word used for someone or something, either as a COMMON NOUN (**book**, **courage**) or a PROPER NOUN (**Suzuki, Haida Gwaii**)

noun clause: a THAT-CLAUSE (*I know **that it's late**.*) or a WH-CLAUSE (*I didn't know **what you were doing**.*) used like a NOUN PHRASE

noun phrase: a phrase in which the main word is a NOUN and which is used as a SUBJECT or an OBJECT (***Their new condo** is really big so they're having **a party** for **sixty people** on **Saturday night**.*)

object: a NOUN, NOUN PHRASE, or PRONOUN used as a DIRECT OBJECT (*He took **the money**.*), INDIRECT OBJECT (*I gave **him** the money.*), or after a PREPOSITION (*He took it with **him**.*)

object pronoun: a PERSONAL PRONOUN (**me, you, him, her, it, us, them**) used as an OBJECT (*James gave **them** to **me**, not **her**.*)

pair noun: a NOUN used for something made of two matching parts such as **scissors** or **pants**.

parenthetical noun clause: a NOUN CLAUSE used after a NOUN to provide extra information, typically set off by commas, dashes, or parentheses (*His first suggestion, **that we should go to Red Deer**, wasn't very popular.*)

participle: a VERB form, either the PRESENT PARTICIPLE (**breaking, repairing**) or the PAST PARTICIPLE (**broken, repaired**)

participle adjective: an ADJECTIVE derived from a PRESENT PARTICIPLE (**surprising**) or a PAST PARTICIPLE (**shocked**) (*She seemed **shocked** by the **surprising** news.*)

participle clause = reduced adverbial clause

particle: a PREPOSITION (**on**) or ADVERB (**away**) combined with a VERB to make a PHRASAL VERB (*He put **on** his jacket and walked **away**.*)

passive: a VERB form with **be** plus the PAST PARTICIPLE of a TRANSITIVE VERB, used to describe what happens to the SUBJECT (*My car **was stolen**.*); compare ACTIVE

past participle: a VERB form such as **broken** or **repaired**, used in the PERFECT (*I had **broken** my watch.*) and the PASSIVE (*It was **repaired**.*)

Past Perfect: a VERB form using **had** + PAST PARTICIPLE (***Had** you **forgotten** anything?*)

Past Progressive: a VERB form using **was** or **were** + PRESENT PARTICIPLE (*The baby **was sleeping**.*)

percentage: a phrase such as **ten percent** (**10%**) used as a QUANTIFIER with **of** before a DETERMINER or PRONOUN to describe a part of something (***Ten percent** of the population is living in poverty.*)

perfect: a VERB form using **have** + PAST PARTICIPLE (***Have** you **forgotten** anything?*)

personal pronoun: one of the SUBJECT PRONOUNS (**I, you, he, she, it, we, they**) or OBJECT PRONOUNS (**me, you, him, her, it, us, them**)

personification: the treatment of an abstract idea or a thing as if it was a person (***Death's cold hand touched his shoulder**.*)

phrasal modal: a phrase such **as be able to, be going to**, or **have to**, used instead of a MODAL (*We **have to** wait for Cathy.*); compare MODAL

phrasal verb: a VERB + PARTICLE combination such as **sleep in** or **put on** (*He **put on** his shoes.*)

Pluperfect = Past Perfect

possessive: a word such as **my, your**, or **their** used as a DETERMINER before a NOUN (**my chair, your money**) and **mine, yours**, or **theirs** used as a PRONOUN instead of a NOUN PHRASE (*I found **mine**, but I couldn't find **yours**.*)

possessive determiner: my, your, his, her, its, our, their; compare POSSESSIVE PRONOUN

possessive noun: a NOUN plus an apostrophe with **s** (**Lee's car**) or without s (**The Weakerthans' first CD**)

possessive pronoun: **mine, yours, his, hers, ours, theirs;** compare POSSESSIVE DETERMINER

predicative adjective: an ADJECTIVE used after a LINKING VERB (*Her hair was **red** and her eyes were **green**.*); compare ATTRIBUTIVE ADJECTIVE

predictive conditional = first conditional

preposition: a word such as **at** or **on**, or a phrase such as **in front of**, used before a NOUN, NOUN PHRASE, or PRONOUN in a PREPOSITIONAL PHRASE (*I'll meet you **at** noon **on** Friday **in front of** the library.*)

prepositional phrase: a PREPOSITION plus a NOUN, NOUN PHRASE, or PRONOUN (**on the table, in front of me**)

present participle: a VERB form such as **sleeping**, used in the PROGRESSIVE (*Is he **sleeping**?*); compare **past participle**

Present Perfect: a VERB form using **has** or **have** + PAST PARTICIPLE (***Have** you **forgotten** anything?*)

Present Progressive: a VERB form using **am, is,** or **are** + PRESENT PARTICIPLE (*The baby **is sleeping**.*)

progressive: a VERB form using **be** + PRESENT PARTICIPLE (*The baby **is sleeping**.*)

pronoun: a word such as **she, anything,** or **herself** used instead of a NOUN or NOUN PHRASE (*Jaunita is very old and **she** can't do **anything** by **herself**.*)

proper noun: a NOUN with a capital letter used as the name of someone or something (***Elsa** is from **Switzerland**.*); compare COMMON NOUN

quantifier: a word such as **many** and **some** or a phrase such as **a few** and **a lot (of)** used to refer to quantities (***Some** people have **a lot of** money.*)

question: a sentence with an AUXILIARY VERB before the SUBJECT and MAIN VERB, used as a WH-QUESTION (*When did he leave?*) or a YES/NO QUESTION (*Did he leave?*)

question tag: an AUXILIARY VERB plus a SUBJECT PRONOUN used as a short form of a QUESTION added after a statement (*He hasn't left yet, **has he**? He's still here, **isn't he**?*)

quotation marks: a pair of marks ("...") inside which we put DIRECT SPEECH, special words or phrases, and some titles (*"I'm tired," he said.*) (*Have you read "In Flanders Fields"?*)

real conditional: a type of CONDITIONAL in which the events happen, have happened, or are likely to happen (*If I open the door, the cat will run out.*); compare UNREAL CONDITIONAL

reciprocal pronoun: **each other** and **one another**, used when an action or feeling goes both ways between people or things (*My brothers avoid **each other** whenever possible.*)

reduced adverbial clause: an ADVERBIAL CLAUSE formed with a PARTICIPLE or a SUBORDINATING CONJUNCTION plus a PARTICIPLE (***(Before) leaving the house**, he turned off the lights.*)

reduced negative: a short form of a NEGATIVE, typically formed with a CONJUNCTION plus **not** (*Do you want this **or not**? **If not**, can I have it?*)

reduced relative clause: a RELATIVE CLAUSE formed with a PARTICIPLE and no RELATIVE PRONOUN (*I saw some people **waiting outside**.*)

reflexive pronoun: **myself, yourself, himself, herself, itself, ourselves, yourselves,** and **themselves**, used when the OBJECT of the VERB is the same person or thing as the SUBJECT of the verb (*He burned **himself** cooking dinner.*)

relative clause: a CLAUSE typically introduced by a RELATIVE PRONOUN and used to provide additional information about a NOUN PHRASE in a preceding CLAUSE (*I was on a bus **that was packed with children who were making a lot of noise.***)

relative pronoun: the words **who, whom, which,** and **that** used to introduce a RELATIVE CLAUSE (*I have a friend **who** can fix computers.*)

reported speech = indirect speech

reporting verb: a VERB such as **say** or **reply** used with DIRECT SPEECH (*He **said,** "Hello."*) or INDIRECT SPEECH (*I **replied** that I was busy.*)

rhetorical question: a sentence in the form of a QUESTION used to make a statement. (*Who cares?*)

second conditional: a type of UNREAL CONDITIONAL used to express a distant and unlikely connection between one imaginary event and another (*If I had a lot of money, I'd buy a Mercedes.*)

simple preposition: a PREPOSITION that is a single word such as **at, during, in,** or **without**; compare COMPLEX PREPOSITION

simple sentence: a single CLAUSE with a SUBJECT and a VERB (*Mary sneezed.*), which may also include an OBJECT and an ADVERBIAL (*We ate lunch in a café.*); compare COMPOUND SENTENCE and COMPLEX SENTENCE

split infinitive: an INFINITIVE with an ADVERB between **to** and the VERB (*I want **to really understand** him.*)

stative verb: a VERB used to describe a state, not an action (*I **know** that he **has** a lot of money.*); compare ACTION VERB

subject: a NOUN, NOUN PHRASE, or PRONOUN typically used before a VERB to identify who or what performs the action of the VERB (***Tony** lost his keys and **I** found them.*)

subject pronoun: a PERSONAL PRONOUN (**I, you, he, she, it, we, they**) used as SUBJECT (***He** wants to get married and **she** doesn't.*)

subject-verb agreement: the relationship of a singular SUBJECT with a singular VERB (***He is** eating lunch.*) or a plural SUBJECT with a plural verb (***They are** eating lunch.*)

subjunctive: a special use of the BASE FORM of a VERB in a NOUN CLAUSE, sometimes called the present subjunctive (*They have proposed that taxes **be** increased.*); also the use of **were** in a NOUN CLAUSE after the VERB **wish** (*I wish I **were** older.*) and in a HYPOTHETICAL CONDITIONAL (*If I **were** you, I'd complain.*), sometimes called the past subjunctive

subordinating conjunction: a word or phrase used to introduce an ADVERBIAL CLAUSE (**because**), a NOUN CLAUSE (**that**), or a RELATIVE CLAUSE (**who**) (*I didn't know **that** you were the person **who** called me **because** you didn't leave your name.*); compare COORDINATING CONJUNCTION

substitution: the use of words such as **one, ones, so,** and **do so** instead of repeating a word, phrase, or CLAUSE (*I have a black pen, but I need a red **one**.*)

summary report: a short report using a VERB that summarizes what was said (*He apologized.*)

superlative: an ADJECTIVE or ADVERB with **-est** (**fastest**) or **most/least** (**most expensive**) after **the**, used to say that something has the most or the least of a quality (*He wants to get **the fastest** and **most expensive** car in the world.*); compare COMPARATIVE

tag question = question tag

tense: the relationship between the VERB form and the time of the action or state it describes

that-clause: a type of NOUN CLAUSE beginning with **that** (*I thought **that I had made a mistake**.*)

third conditional: a type of UNREAL CONDITIONAL used to describe an imaginary connection between two events that never happened (*If you had been born in the Middle Ages, you would have had a harsh life.*)

three-word verb: a PHRASAL VERB plus a PREPOSITION (*You should **hold on to** that book.*)

transitive verb: a VERB used with an OBJECT (*I **dropped** the ball.*); compare INTRANSITIVE VERB

two-word verb = phrasal verb

uncountable noun: a NOUN that can only be singular and is used to refer to things such as activities (**research**), ideas (**honesty**), and substances (**rice**), but not separate individuals; compare COUNTABLE NOUN

unreal conditional: a type of CONDITIONAL in which the events have not happened, are not likely to happen, or are imaginary (*If you had asked me earlier, I would have helped you.*); compare REAL CONDITIONAL

verb: a word used in a CLAUSE to describe the action (**eat, steal**) or state (**belong, understand**) of the SUBJECT (*He **stole** something that **belonged** to me.*)

verb with object = transitive verb

verb without object = intransitive verb

wh-clause: a type of NOUN CLAUSE beginning with a WH-WORD such as **what** or **whether** (*I don't know **what she wants**. I can't remember **whether she likes tea or coffee**.*)

wh-cleft: a structure in which a sentence (*I'm not supposed to drink coffee.*) is divided into two parts, one part as a CLAUSE typically beginning with **What** (*What I'm not supposed to drink*) and the other part **be** + an emphasized element (*What I'm not supposed to drink is coffee.*); compare IT-CLEFT

wh-question: a QUESTION beginning with **What, Who, When, How much**, etc. (***When** did he leave?*); compare YES/NO QUESTION

wh-word: a word such as **what, who, where, how much**, etc. used at the beginning of a WH-QUESTION or a WH-CLAUSE (***Where** have you been?*)(*I don't know **what's** wrong.*)

yes/no question: a QUESTION beginning with an AUXILIARY VERB or **be**, typically answered with **yes** or **no**. (*Did he leave?*); compare WH-QUESTION

zero conditional: a type of REAL CONDITIONAL used to express a fixed connection between two events now, in the past, or always (*If the fruit is soft, it's ready to eat.*)

Answer key

Pages 2–3

A 1 Agecoutay ran to the scene of the accident. (line 13) OR Emergency responders called the teenager a hero. (line 27)

2 After Agecoutay had pulled the girl to safety, he wrapped her in his own jacket while they waited for an ambulance, which showed up a few minutes later. (line 23)

B 1 after
2 fell
3 and
4 pull
5 After
6 wrapped
7 Because

Pages 4–5

A 1 won't be easy
2 Was *Lord of the Flies*
3 has pockets
4 doesn't interest me
5 isn't going to
6 None of you are
7 have I had
8 wasn't about dancing
9 Is Statistics
10 aren't made

B 1 was (c)
2 was (e)
3 is (a)
4 are (d)
5 is (b)

C 1 orchestra have
2 everybody has
3 Nobody ... has
4 committee have
5 Marbles has
6 teachers has/have
7 police have
8 eggs has

Pages 6–7

A 1 suitcase
2 carry things
3 travel (OR are travelling)
4 hinge
5 swings
6 closes
7 hallucination
8 seeing things
9 hypocrite
10 pretends
11 behaves
12 hijacker
13 seizes
14 go
15 demand things

B 1 take (b) put it in
2 like (c) going to
3 wait (d) shivering
4 heard (a) believe it

C 1 gets, moves
2 rest, nap (OR nap, rest)
3 hibernate, eat
4 lie, fall
5 talks, happens
6 sing, go
7 snore, breathe

Pages 8–9

A 1 She whispered "Good luck" to him.

2 The judge fined her $500 for her actions.

3 The farmer refused us permission to walk across his field (OR refused to give us permission OR refused to give permission to us)

4 Juan confessed (to me) that he took (OR had taken) Caroline's book.

B 1 reserved ... keeping it for
2 transmitted ... spread them to (OR spread ... transmit them to)
3 retrieved ... found them for (OR found ... retrieved them for)
4 traded ... sells him to (OR sold ... trades him to)
5 required ... offer them to

C She explained us > She explained to us (OR She explained);
gave the following information half of the husbands > information to half;
Your wife has described you a trip to China > described a trip to China to you;
One of her friends told to her > told her;
You think sounds like a really good idea > think (that) it sounds;
you ask to her some questions > ask her some questions (OR ask some questions);
Your wife has suggested you a trip to China > suggested a trip to China to you;
You don't like > You don't like it;
You believe is a really bad idea > You believe (that) it is a really bad idea;
you ask some questions her > ask her some questions (OR ask some questions);
The researcher didn't tell to the wives > tell the wives;
the wives she said to the husbands > the wives what she said;
decide the husbands thought it was a good idea > decide if (OR whether) the husbands thought

Pages 10–11

A 1 Soon there **were** all kinds of forms available from Bullnotes ... (line 41)
OR The big problem, they soon discovered, **is** that everyone wants these things ... (line 45)
OR In what turned out to **be** a common experience ... (line 48)
OR ... and there really won't **be** a problem with the letter of application. (line 60)

2 **Be:** For several years he **will have been** trying to turn a good idea… (line 3)
OR He won't **be** doing anything special … (line 5)
OR They **were** starting to make a small steady profit when they met Terry Lloyd. (line 18)
OR Terry had **been** creating home pages for his friends … (line 20)
OR They soon found that students **were** looking for more than lecture notes. (line 26)
OR They needed to do other things that they **weren't** learning in their classes. (line 27)
OR Imagine that you **are** applying for a scholarship. (line 29)
OR You have **been** trying to write a letter of application and you can't get it right. (line 30)
OR You need an example of the kind of letter you **are** trying to write. (line 31)
OR "I **am** writing this letter …" (line 36)
OR Dylan **was** working day and night … (line 43)
OR … he didn't think about what he **was** doing in terms of a business (line 44)
OR Dylan **is** still looking for a way to make Bullnotes work as a business, but these days he is always counting his pennies and he is having a hard time paying his bills. (line 52)
Choose one: For several years he will **have** been trying … (line 3)
OR … his business venture won't **have** made any money for most of the past year. (line 7)
OR When they started, it **had** seemed like such a great idea. (line 11)
OR Dylan and his friend, Michael Underwood, **had** been writing up their lecture notes … (line 12)
OR They **had** used that money to pay … (line 15)
OR Terry **had** been creating home pages for his friends … (line 20)
OR You **have** been trying to write a letter of application and you can't get it right. (line 30)
OR Or maybe someone **has** asked you to write a letter of recommendation. (line 33)
OR … whom I **have** known for … (line 38)
OR He **has** thought about taking a teaching job … (line 57)
In the following examples, *have* is a main verb, not an auxiliary verb:
they **had** a successful website … (line 50)
OR … he is **having** a hard time paying his bills. (line 57)
OR He **has** lots of experience now … (line 60)

B 1 B
2 E
3 D
4 A
5 C

C **Choose one from each list.**
Imperative or infinitive: turn (A), celebrate (A), do (A, B, C), pay (B, D), make (B, D, E), become (B), Imagine (C), write (C), get (C), download (C), be (D), create (D), work (E)
Simple Present: need (C)
Simple Present + s in third person singular: is (A), wants (D), has (E)
Present Progressive: are applying (C), am writing (C), is (always) counting (E), is having (E)
Present Perfect: has asked (C), have known (C), has thought (E)
Present Perfect Progressive: have been trying (C)
Simple Past: started (B), sold (B), met (B), showed (B), created (B), established (B), set (B), found (C), needed (C), were (D), didn't think (D), discovered (D), turned (D), tried (D), had (D), didn't (really) make (D), went (E), was (D)
Past Progressive: were starting (B), were looking (C), weren't learning (C), was working (D), was doing (D)
Past Perfect: had seemed (B), had used (B)
Past Perfect Progressive: had been writing (B), (had been) selling (B), had been creating (B)
Future: will (soon) need (A), won't be (E), will have (A)
Future Progressive: won't be doing (A)
Future Perfect: won't have made (A)
Future Perfect Progressive: will have been trying (A)

Pages 12–13

A 1 is being
2 tell
3 says
4 has
5 is
6 look
7 are
8 live
9 move
10 resemble
11 'm (OR am) looking
12 isn't
13 Do … know
14 're (OR are) fixing
15 's (OR is) using

B 1 has won … has said … hat trick
2 also-ran … has taken … has not finished
3 has heard … has-been … has trained

4 no-show ... has bought ...
   hasn't come

C 1 have ... known (c) 've
   (OR have) been
2 (b) 've (OR have) ... been
   swimming
3 Have ... completed (d) 've
   (OR have) done
4 Have ... shown (a) 's (OR
   has) been reading

D She is living here since 2009 >
   She's (OR She has) lived OR
   She's (OR She has) been living;
   she has been going back >
   she's (OR she has) gone back;
   She's having an accent >
   She has an accent;
   people who are coming from
   France > people who come
   from France;
   I never ask her > I've (OR I
   have) never asked her;
   if she is speaking French >
   if she speaks French;
   She is really liking to go to the
   theatre > She really likes to go;
   she is inviting me > she's
   (OR she has) invited me
   OR she invited me;
   In the short time I am
   knowing her > I've (OR I
   have) known her;
   we become good friends >
   we've (OR we have) become
   good friends

Pages 14–15

A 1 were listening
2 came
3 said
4 were making
5 broke
6 stole
7 was teaching
8 saw
9 explained
10 understood
11 was talking
12 didn't get
13 missed
14 was wondering
   (OR wondered)

B 1 had been worrying
   (OR had worried)

2 had planned (OR had
   been planning)
3 had been
4 had broken
5 had caught
6 had been living
   (OR had lived)
7 had been taking
   (OR removing)
8 had made
9 had ... removed
   (OR taken)
10 had ... had

C we sometimes stop > we
   sometimes stopped (OR we
   would sometimes stop);
   If it wasn't rain > raining;
   we just sleep outside > we just
   slept (OR we would just sleep);
   We really enjoying that >
   enjoyed;
   If it was rain > was raining
   (OR rained);
   and crawl inside > crawled;
   while we sleep in the tent >
   were sleeping;
   I think > thought;
   the ground moving under me
   > was moving (OR moved);
   I sit up > sat;
   and I realize > realized;
   the tent was try to move >
   was trying;
   was hold it in place > was
   holding;
   When we get outside > got;
   we discover > discovered;
   that we stand > were standing;
   our tent slowly floats away >
   was slowly floating;
   we really surprised > we were
   really surprised;
   then we think > thought;
   it is very funny > was

Pages 16–17

A 1 we should never (line 6)
   OR don't have to (line 48)
   OR won't (line 64)
2 We **may** be told, for
   example, that we **should**
   never open an umbrella
   indoors because that **will**
   bring bad luck. (line 6)

B 1 E
2 C
3 D
4 A
5 B

C We aren't told why or what
   kind of bad thing **might**
   happen to us, but few of us **are
   going to** try to find out. (line 8)
   Others **will** say that seeing a
   black cat **is supposed to** be
   lucky. (line 38)
   This is usually heard when
   people talk about their good
   luck or when they are hoping
   that they **will be able to** get
   or do something they want.
   (line 53)

Pages 18–19

A 1 can't (OR cannot OR
   aren't able to) fly ... can
   (OR are able to) ...
   swimming
2 unflappable ... can
   (OR is able to) stay
3 numb ... couldn't
   (OR wasn't able to) feel
4 illiterate ... can't
   (OR cannot OR aren't
   able to) read
5 successful ... been able to
   ... tried OR has tried
6 managed ... were able to
   ... difficult

B 1 couldn't
2 could
3 could
4 can

C 1 may (c)
2 be allowed to (f)
3 Can (a)
4 be allowed to (e)
5 can (or may) (b)
6 be allowed to (d)

D Of course, you could > you can;
   she isn't being able to do her
   own work > she isn't able to
   (OR she can't do);
   she can have said > she could
   have said (OR she can say);
   Sorry, but you can not > can't
   (OR cannot);

how do they could do their
work … ? > how could they
do their work … ? (OR how
can they do their work … ?);
I knew that I can have tried >
could have tried;
I didn't think I'll can change
how she behaved > I didn't
think I could change

Pages 20–21

A 1 may have … absurd
2 may be … disqualified
3 undecided … may …
may not
4 potential … might not
5 may not … feasible
6 theoretical … might

B 1 can pick
2 can't imagine
3 could be
4 couldn't be sent
5 could have been avoided
6 could have been saved

C 1 They ~~can~~ be going to >
may / might / could
2 Someone ~~can~~ still be using
> may / might / could
3 You ~~may~~ be hanged >
might / could
4 These people ~~can~~ have >
may / might
5 I ~~can~~ have finished > may
/ might / could … I ~~can~~
not > may / might
6 ~~May~~ someone tell me >
Can / Could
7 we really ~~might not~~ believe
> can't / cannot / could
not / couldn't
8 if you ~~may~~ be willing
> might
9 the weather ~~can~~ be > may
/ might / could
10 ~~May~~ the children > Could

Pages 22–23

A 1 extra … don't have to
2 step … have to
3 fruit … mustn't
4 must / have to …
command
5 obligation … don't have to
6 duty-free … don't have to

7 taboo … mustn't
8 evil … have to

B 1 didn't have to … required
2 didn't need to …
unnecessary
3 must not … allowed
4 need to … official
5 having to … significant
6 must … impossible

C 1 so you must not clean
them > don't have to clean
2 Everyone will have got to
go > will have to go
3 I'll need get some
medicine > I'll need to get
(OR I'll have to get)
4 I must to find a
replacement > I must find
(OR I have to find)
5 customers don't need leave
> don't need to leave
6 we had got to take a taxi >
we had to take
7 the one to must have to
tell him > the one to have
to tell him (OR the one
who must (OR has to)
tell him)
8 you don't need be over
eighteen > you don't need
to (OR have to) be
9 we must go > we had to go
10 we didn't need wait > we
didn't need to wait

Pages 24–25

A will find (line 28); were found
(line 42); have been moving
(line 23); had been moved
(line 16)

B 1 have been … injured
2 have been left
3 was hit
4 were (OR have been)
destroyed
5 were (OR have been)
buried / trapped
6 have blocked
7 have had to be flown in
8 are going to be felt

C 1 the apple blossoms that
are always **shaken** loose
from the trees (line 4) OR

and **(are) blown** along the
country roads (line 6) OR
The scenes of devastation
this morning **are**
described by one rescue
worker as "like the end of
the world" (line 21)
2 The names of all victims
are being withheld until
their families can be
notified (line 47)
3 For as long as people can
remember, small towns …
have been hit by storms
every spring (line 1)
OR … the roads **have**
been blocked by dozens
of fallen trees (line 26) OR
About 100 people **have**
been seriously **injured**
(line 50) OR more than
1000 **have been left**
homeless (line 51)
4 the Clintons **were found**
alive by rescuers this
morning (line 42) OR
Tragically, they **were**
both **killed** when part
of a wall crashed through
the floor on top of them.
(line 45)
5 Other buildings where
tractors and equipment
were being stored seem
to have been completely
blown away. (line 18)
6 Herds of cattle that **had**
been moved into barns
for safety are nowhere to
be seen, nor are the barns.
(line 16)

Pages 26–27

A 1 Narmatha was seen
outside the theatre as
she was waiting to go in.
She had a new hairstyle.
2 Karen feels sad because
she wasn't promoted (OR
hasn't been promoted)
and she has to pretend
as if nothing happened.
3 The puck is passed to
Palmeri (OR Palmeri is
passed the puck). Palmeri

tries to go past Jennings, but she is stopped (by Jennings).

B 1 impossible (a)
2 inexplicable (b)
3 knowledgeable (b)
4 illegible (b)
5 inaudible (a)
6 unspeakable (b)
7 reusable (a), (b)

C just after my younger sister born > was born;
Lots of people were come > came;
I gave the job > was given;
As each guest was arrived > arrived;
I handed boxes > was handed;
which filled with things > were filled;
that wrapped in Christmas paper > were wrapped;
I told which ones > was told;
and which ones had to be place > had to be placed (OR I had to place);
So many presents brought for us > were brought;
the experience of given so much > being given

Pages 28–29

A what is done, not who does it (1)
we don't know … who performed the actions (2)
the person or thing affected by the action (3)
that subject is the topic of two or more sentences (5)
several actions that affect the same subject in a single sentence (4)
rules and warning notices (9)
procedures, especially in research reports (7)
formal written reports (8)
to avoid personal commands (11)
to avoid implying that we are only referring to ourselves (10)
the speaker of statements and questions (13)
of orders and requests in

infinitives (12)
to distance ourselves from the reported information (14)
not sure if the information is reliable (15)
a current report (17)
a report of something in the past (18)

B You can only consult reference books in the library.
You must obtain special permission to use them outside the library.
You should return all books on time or you will have to pay a fine.
If you do not pay the fine, you will lose borrowing rights.
You may not borrow library books for others or give them to others.
If you lose a book, you must pay the cost of replacement.

C 1 are (OR were) said to be
2 were told not to use
3 is (OR was) reported to have died
4 wasn't mentioned … were received

D It has been claimed that tasks cannot be used successfully with beginner level students. The following study was designed so that that claim could be investigated.
Two groups of students were created, each with different proficiency levels.
They were given a task in which they were shown a set of pictures and asked to tell a story. (OR A task was given to them … a set of pictures was shown to them … they were asked)
They were recorded as they spoke and then their stories were examined.

Pages 30–31

A 1 True
2 False
3 False
4 False

5 True
6 True
7 False
8 True

B 1 an entrance (line 32)
2 the Arctic (line 37)

C 1 the Arctic (line 37)
2 Inuit (line 1)
3 an igloo (line 1), a skill (line 1), a description (line 5), a saw (line 10), a circle (line 10), a slope (line 19), a spiral (line 28), a dome (line 29), a cylinder (line 29), an entrance (line 32), a … place (line 36), a night (line 37)
4 the process (line 4), the circle (line 14), the bottom (line 15), the top (line 16), The slope (line 20), the … block (line 20), the igloo (line 27), the centre (line 29), the … piece (line 30), the saw (line 32), the entrance (line 33)
5 generation (line 3)
6 the edges (line 17), the blocks (line 17), the tops (line 19)
7 blocks (line 26)
8 The snow (line 9), the ground (line 21)
9 snow (line 7)

Pages 32–33

A when we first mention them (1)
when we think they are already known (2)
when we classify the kind of thing we're referring to (3)
any example of the kind of thing we're referring to (4)
the work they do (6)
the kind of beliefs they have (5)
in definitions (9)
in descriptions of particular features (8)
the type of thing mentioned (7)
the same ordinary things as we are in our daily lives (11)
in the physical world outside (10)

identify people by their jobs (12)

their unique roles in society (14)

with professional organizations (13)

inventions and musical instruments (16)

in generalizations (15)

prepositional phrases with **of** (19)

relative clauses (18)

superlative adjectives and emphasizing adjectives such as **main** or **first** (17)

B
1 the
2 the
3 Ø
4 a
5 a
6 Ø
7 the
8 an
9 a
10 the
11 the
12 the
13 a
14 a
15 a
16 Ø
17 Ø
18 a

C
1 (f) the
2 (d) a
3 (a) the
4 (e) a (OR the)
5 (c) a
6 (b) the

D
1 a
2 the
3 Ø
4 a
5 the
6 Ø
7 a
8 the
9 Ø
10 The
11 a
12 Ø

E I was starting to learn the English > learn English;
He was from London in the Ontario > in Ontario;
He was always making the jokes > making jokes;
One day he wrote words > wrote the words;
on blackboard > on the blackboard;
I offered to answer question > answer the question;
changed to the A > changed to A (OR an A);
that was good answer > that was a good answer;
he changed letter > changed the letter;
happy with new spelling > happy with the new spelling;
with the absolute confidence > with absolute confidence;
I looked around in the confusion > in confusion;
it needed second M > needed a second M;
it should have the M too > an M;
nodded with the smile > with a smile;
I still remember terrible feeling > I still remember the terrible feeling;
feeling of the embarrassment > of embarrassment

Pages 34–35

A
1 a
2 a
3 a
4 one
5 a
6 a
7 a
8 a
9 Ø
10 Ø
11 a
12 Ø
13 a
14 one
15 a
16 a

B
1 an
2 Ø
3 Ø
4 Ø
5 Ø
6 an
7 Ø
8 a
9 a
10 a
11 Ø
12 Ø
13 a (OR the)
14 Ø
15 the
16 the (OR Ø)
17 Ø
18 Ø
19 the
20 the
21 Ø
22 Ø
23 Ø
24 a
25 Ø
26 the
27 Ø
28 the
29 the
30 Ø

C
1 Ø
2 Ø
3 a
4 a
5 one
6 one
7 an (OR Ø)
8 Ø
9 a (OR one)
10 one
11 the
12 a (OR the)
13 the (OR a)
14 a
15 the
16 the
17 the
18 a
19 the
20 the
21 a
22 Ø (OR one-)
23 the
24 an
25 an
26 the
27 the
28 the
29 Ø
30 Ø

Pages 36–37

A people, animals, and objects (1)
actions and events (2)
substances and materials (5)
abstract ideas, qualities,
and states (4)
activities (3)
a single thing (7)
a substance or general idea (8)
in phrases which are
countable (10)
separate units or parts of nouns
which are uncountable (9)

B 1 government
2 a country
3 a ... piece
4 toast
5 Ø ... bread
6 soup
7 a mixture
8 cereal (OR nuts)
9 nuts (OR cereal)
10 Ø ... fruit
11 milk
12 breakfast

C 1 outskirts ... are (e)
2 press is (d)
3 clergy are (f)
4 Mathematics is (b)
5 Binoculars are (a)
6 is (c) fortnight

Pages 38–39

A 1 all these changes (line 27)
2 all cars (lines 11, 17, 53)

B 1 C
2 E
3 D
4 A
5 B

C 1 That car (line 16)
this area (line 20)
those old farms (line 23)
OR those Saturday trips
(line 37)
these changes (line 27)
2 **Choose one from four
of these sets**:
my grandfather (lines 1, 5,
30, 39) OR my
grandmother (lines 2, 7,
27) OR my eyes (line 3)

OR my grandparents
(lines 19, 26) OR my
driveway (line 50);
their voices (line 4) OR
their lifetimes (line 20);
our return (line 37) OR
our accident (line 38) OR
our driveway (lines 42, 45);
his thoughts (line 43) OR
his window (line 48);
your house (line 51)

Pages 40–41

A 1 a little, much
2 each, every, one
3 a few, both, many, several,
ten

B 1 **Choose four:**
a lot of other cars (line 8)
Both of my grandparents
(line 19)
lots of new houses (line 23)
one of them (line 26)
some of the problems
(line 31)
one of those Saturday
trips (line 37)

C 1 these
2 my
3 those
4 his
5 this
6 that
7 our
8 a few
9 much
10 the
11 his
12 some
13 some
14 seventy-five
15 most
16 a little
17 a
18 both
19 each
20 half

D 1 minority ... a few
2 maximum ... much
3 quota ... many
4 unanimous ... every
5 lottery ... any
6 majority ... most

E One of boys fell > One of
the boys;
twisted the ankle badly >
twisted his ankle;
Most them stayed > Most
of them;
with injured boy > with the
injured boy;
while two the older boys left >
two of the older boys;
this two boys didn't know >
these two boys;
walking around in big circle >
in a big circle;
for a few hour > a few hours;
back with his friends > their
friends;
each boys had brought some
water > each boy (OR each
of the boys);
all them managed to survive
> all of them (OR they all)
managed

Pages 42–43

A with plural and uncountable
nouns (1)
as pronouns (2)
referring to something
specific (3)
in positive sentences (5)
in questions or offers expecting
positive answers (4)
in sentences with a negative
element (7)
in questions when no specific
answer is expected (6)
in **if**-clauses (9)
"it doesn't matter which
one" (8)
a large amount or number (10)
an approximate number or
percentage (12)
a person, place, or thing
whose identity is unknown (11)
to emphasize "not any" (13)
before subject nouns (14)
before singular and plural
nouns (16)
as a pronoun and with **of**-
phrases (15)

B 1 (c) any
2 (f) any
3 (b) no

4 (e) any

5 (a) some

6 (d) some

C 1 There was some woman here yesterday asking if we had any old clothes, but I told her we didn't (have any).

2 Some (OR Some of the) information in that newspaper article was incorrect. There aren't any wolves or bears on Pelee Island.

3 I've managed to find some dry paper to start a fire, but I can't light it. Don't you have any matches?

4 I'm sure I made some mistakes when I was typing. If you find any mistakes, please correct them.

D 1 some
2 no
3 any
4 some
5 any
6 no
7 some
8 any
9 no
10 any

E 1 empty … none
2 uninhabited … some … none
3 some … any … extinct
4 no … scoreless
5 dead … no

Pages 44–45

A 1 **it's** as if you've known each other all your lives (line 25)

2 **She** took his right hand and placed it against hers, palms touching (line 32)

B 1 D
2 C
3 E
4 A
5 B

C 1 They, we (C)
2 hers, mine, yours* (E)

*Note that **his** in **his right hand** (E) is a determiner, not a pronoun.

Pages 46–47

A You meet **someone** for the first time, and it's as if you've known each other all your lives. (line 24) **Everything** goes smoothly. (line 26)

B 1 yours
2 they
3 his
4 it … him
5 that … this

C 1 You know that you shouldn't use a phone while you're driving.

2 I heard that they're going to demolish this old factory so (that) they can build a new school.

3 If you're self-indulgent, you allow yourself to do or have too much of what you like.

4 I think that we shouldn't criticize when we're not sure of our facts. (OR I think that you shouldn't criticize when you're not sure of your facts.)

D 1 A disguise … something … no one

2 Camouflage … something … everything

3 A mirage … something … nothing

E she played it > played them; for we to learn the words > for us; hers favourite songs > her; no really understood the words > no one (OR nobody); but every talked > everyone (OR everybody); about different something > about something different; in his groups > their; And no ones were > no one (OR nobody) was; were trying > was; one song that went like that > this;

what your want > you; what your need > you; That was interesting words > Those were; I did learn somethings > something (OR some things)

Pages 48–49

A 1 very important (line 15) OR really bad (line 34)

2 large heavy wooden wardrobes (line 33)

B 1 best
2 very (OR really)
3 important
4 diagonally
5 directly
6 horizontal
7 small
8 large (OR heavy OR wooden)
9 pointed
10 Blue
11 soft
12 natural

C Restrictive: main (line 16) Intensifying: perfect (line 5)

D **Choose one example of each type.**
Opinion: comfortable, harmonious, beneficial, important, best, better, easier, bad, vulnerable, restless, negative, soothing, peaceful
Size: small, large
Physical Quality: heavy, soft
Age or Time: ancient, modern, contemporary
Shape: pointed, horizontal
Colour: blue, brown

E **Choose one example of each type.**
Location: outdoor
Origin or Source: Chinese
Material: wooden
Type: agricultural, physical, horizontal, natural
Purpose: relaxing

Pages 50–51

A **Choose two:** ancient Chinese OR large wooden OR heavy wooden OR soft natural

B 1 The flags of Britain and the US both have red, white(,) **and** blue designs.

2 He described the wonderful, friendly, outgoing people who worked in the little Italian café.

3 You immediately notice the large plastic vases with pink **and** purple flowers on every table.

4 There are many industrial **and** agricultural applications of the new chemical compounds.

5 What are the cultural, religious(,) **and** historic origins of these current regional conflicts?

C 1 The entire soccer team played well.

2 The wine made a small red stain.

3 There's nothing new in our main cultural values.

4 You'll need comfortable leather hiking boots.

5 It has a long pointed stem with tiny pink flowers.

6 The windows are in huge circular wooden frames.

7 They are the major northern industrial nations.

8 ✓

9 They found a beautiful antique rocking chair.

10 Her mother was alone in the total chaos.

11 ✓

12 We like recent Canadian economic policies.

D 1 large
2 rare
3 black
4 white
5 similar
6 small
7 hard
8 shiny white (OR bluish-grey)
9 bluish-grey (OR shiny white)
10 great

11 thin (OR sharp)
12 sharp (OR thin)
13 cool
14 northern
15 large
16 tropical
17 juicy
18 yellow
19 prickly

E 1 Italian and Greek (OR southern European)
2 great little outdoor
3 carefree, crazy, happy (in any order)
4 older English
5 southern European (OR Italian and Greek)
6 cheap Spanish
7 big square plastic
8 sour and twisted (OR twisted and sour)

Pages 52–53

A 1 We thought we had started our hike early, but other people had already left the campsite (OR had left the campsite already).

2 The workers usually get paid weekly, but they haven't been paid for last week yet (OR they haven't yet been paid for last week).

3 The students still hadn't completed all their work when they had to leave here yesterday.

4 Parvita lived here recently, but she doesn't live here anymore.

5 We used to hardly ever hear them (OR We hardly ever used to hear them), but they've become really noisy lately (OR but lately they've become really noisy).

B 1 always
2 only
3 outside
4 today
5 no longer
6 twice
7 sometimes
8 recently

9 ever
10 yet

C 1 The couple had got married very recently (OR had very recently got married).

2 The baby looks exactly like her mother.

3 He isn't only an athlete, he's a scholar too!

4 Wait for us, we're arriving now.

5 Lunch is almost ready.

6 Wear this crazy hat. It's only for fun.

Pages 54–55

A **Choose four:**
in 1636 (line 8)
In the 1640s (line 13)
From about 1670 (line 19)
to the beginning of the eighteenth century (line 19)
in 1710 (line 23)
for several decades (line 27)
until the Great Expulsion (line 28)
of 1755 (line 29)
in 1763 (line 37)
after the treaty was signed (line 38)
until the twentieth century (line 44)
in the 1920s and 1930s (line 48)

B 1 of
2 in
3 from
4 in
5 from
6 to
7 after
8 between
9 to

C 1 as a result of (b)
2 of whom (a)
3 they worked for OR they had to work for (d)
4 in 1755 (c)

Pages 56–57

A 1 at six in the morning
2 on her birthday next Saturday

3 in September every year
4 at night in winter
5 on Victoria Day in the past
6 at four o'clock on Friday afternoon
7 at sixty-five in 2011
8 on July first in 1867 (OR on the first of July, 1867 OR in 1867 on July first)

B 1 expiry date
2 during
3 deadline
4 in
5 by
6 curfew
7 after
8 at
9 until
10 in

C 1 waiting since an hour > for (OR waiting an hour); till his next meeting > before
2 My sister works > has worked (OR has been working); since after 2010 > since 2010 (OR since before 2010)
3 received in this office until 9 a.m. > by (OR before); in the first of March > on
4 appointments in every morning > appointments every morning; see you on next Monday morning > see you next Monday morning

Pages 58–59

A 1 on (d) in
2 at (c) in
3 in (a) at
4 on (b) in

B 1 The meeting focused **on** economic problems **in** developing countries **in** Southeast Asia.
2 You can either wait **at** the bar or sit **at** a table **in** this restaurant.
3 We were depending **on** my brother to meet us **at** the exit door after the concert.

4 The children were laughing **at** something they had seen **in** a cartoon.

C 1 under … overcoat
2 overpopulation among
3 overlap between
4 overalls over
5 above … overflow
6 below … overhead

Pages 60–61

A helped hundreds of people to stop **smoking** (line 11) and **avoiding** social situations (line 17) situations that will make her want **to smoke** (line 18) many people continue **smoking** (line 23) Encourage her **to avoid** stressful situations (line 25)

B 1 (going) cold turkey (line 34)
2 doing yoga (line 27)
3 kick the habit (line 5)
4 over the counter (line 42)

C 1 want to get (OR want to … be) (2)
2 makes them experience (1)
3 to stop doing (3)
4 of treating (1) (OR for controlling (2) OR without needing (4))

Pages 62–63

A 1 hope (OR am hoping) to visit
2 invited … to stay
3 wants … to spend
4 enjoy taking
5 imagine … making
6 love to be

B 1 allow … to take
2 forget to send
3 meant to clean
4 prefer not to talk (OR prefer not talking)
5 avoid trying to drive
6 forced … to stop playing

C encouraged me take > to take advised me remember > to remember

remember clean the bathrooms > to clean likes clean bathrooms > cleaning (OR to clean) I didn't mind do it > doing I was first starting learn > to learn I could practise speak English > speaking I enjoyed try > trying try improve my English > trying to improve I didn't want work > to work I don't regret do it > doing I decided study harder > to study and try get a better job > to get

Pages 64–65

A 1 He would just nod and **say**, "Thanks for coming by" (line 56)
2 those who had opinions mostly **said** that it was a strange story (line 50)

B 1 C
2 D
3 B
4 F
5 A
6 E

C 1 put (line 10) (OR call out (line 13))
2 grumbled (line 22)

D 1 comma
2 quotation marks
3 comma
4 quotation marks
5 quotation marks
6 quotation marks

E "Karen," Ms. Lee called out, "I'd like you to come and meet Michael." A girl appeared in the doorway. "How do you do?" she said. "Nice to meet you," he mumbled. "Please don't call him 'Michelle' or 'Mikey' or any other silly names," warned Ms. Lee as she swept out of the room. "Look, I drew a picture of the bear from 'Goldilocks,'" Karen suddenly said. "What one?" he asked. "Oh, no, you little Mickey Mouse," she said as she came into the room, "you must say 'Which one?,' not 'What one?,' if you're going to survive here." (OR … into the room. "You must …")

Pages 66–67

A
1 He said that he left (OR had left) his jacket there the day before (OR the previous day).
2 The reviewer wrote that the new book was the funniest thing he or she had ever read.
3 She said that they wouldn't eat it then, but they might have it for lunch the next day (OR the following day).
4 He advised us that we should take as much water as we could carry.
5 You told me that you had to (OR must) get something to eat or you would faint.
6 CompCo is reporting that demand for new computers in Canada is declining.
7 She asked if she should get rid of those old boxes in the closet.

B
1 was
2 could
3 is
4 has
5 are
6 can't
7 won't
8 would
9 will
10 live
11 can
12 lived
13 were
14 had

Pages 68–69

A
1 I mentioned to Mr. Jawal that there was something wrong with the lights.
2 I reminded Julia that she and her friends had to clean up after the party.
3 He warned me (OR you/him/her/us/them) not to touch any of the wires.
4 He denied doing anything wrong. (OR He denied that he had done anything wrong. OR He denied that he did anything wrong. OR He denied having done anything wrong.)

B
1 shouting
2 had mentioned (OR mentioned)
3 wondered
4 talk
5 asked
6 told
7 explained
8 claim
9 begged
10 thought

C I can't agree them > agree with them;
and offered me to help > to help me;
I explained them > explained to them;
that I can't get the wheel off > couldn't;
One of them told that > told me that (or said that);
and assured that > assured me that;
He even suggested me to stand > suggested standing (OR suggested that I (should) stand);
warned me watch out > warned me to watch out (OR warned me that I should watch out);
joked the small wheels > joked about;
I spoke them thanks > I thanked them. (OR I told them, "Thanks" OR I said, "Thanks" to them);
They refused take > refused to take;
I offered pay them > offered to pay them

Pages 70–71

A
1 One of the individuals typically insists **that** he or she will not stop doing something despite the fact **that** it is a source of conflict. (line 46) OR Sometimes one of them will say **that** he or she actually prefers it **that** the other has separate interests. (line 49)
*NOT: On the basis of their study, the researchers have concluded **that** a modern marriage may begin with passionate love, but its survival depends a lot on "companionate love," a feeling that includes affection, caring, and friendship. (line 62)
*In this example, the second **that** (= **which**) is a relative pronoun introducing a relative clause, not a noun clause. See page 74.
2 It makes you wonder **if** getting married is worth the effort. (line 8)

B
1 T
2 T
3 F
4 F
5 F
6 F

C
1 that it was one of their best memories (line 33) OR that he or she will not stop doing something (line 47) OR that he or she actually prefers it that the other has separate interests (line 49)
2 **the case** that marriage has become a gamble (line 10) OR **one indication** that the couple speaks with a single voice (line 25) OR **the fact** that it is a source of conflict (line 48)
3 **likely** that a marriage will end in divorce (line 6) OR **delighted** that so many of their couples

stayed together (line 21) OR **obvious** that these individuals had really different views about marriage (line 57)

4 what advice they would give to younger people thinking about getting married (line 52)

5 **to** what makes a successful marriage (line 14)

Pages 72–73

A 2 We **learned** that pineapples don't grow on trees. (7)

3 No one **noticed** that the keys were missing. (7)

4 She could never **anticipate** what he might want. (8)

5 I'll **show** you how it works. (10)

6 He **screamed** that he hated school. (9) (OR She **said** she felt that everyone was against her. (9) OR He **told** me that he loved me. (10))

7 Donald **suggested** that we should leave early. (8)

8 They **consider** it an offence when women go out in public without covering their heads. (12) (OR We **thought** it odd that no one called us. (13) OR Many people **regard** it as a really bad idea that Parliament approved the bill. (14))

B 1 It doesn't surprise me at all that they don't have any money left.

2 It just astonishes me that children would rather sit watching TV instead of playing outside.

3 It has never been explained why the government didn't act immediately to stop the movement of all animals.

4 It wasn't clear whether Nicole's father had been for or against her marriage, but he did participate in the wedding ceremony.

C 1 what
2 it
3 that
4 that
5 it
6 that
7 Whether
8 that
9 where

D 1 **That** Mr. Lafitte complained about the noise was predictable, but we assured **him** (**that**) it wouldn't happen again. (OR **It was predictable that** Mr. Lafitte complained about the noise, but we assured **him** (**that**) it wouldn't happen again.)

2 The principal warned **us** (OR **me** or **you**) during our meeting **that** some teachers wouldn't like **it that** (OR **the fact that**) their classrooms had suddenly been changed.

3 They told me about **what** Jeff had said, but I thought **it** strange (**that**) he hadn't mentioned money.

4 The police regarded **it as** suspicious **that** the dead woman's husband had recently taken out a life insurance policy in her name.

5 The prosecutor showed the jury how **the crime could** have been committed by Ms. Scott, but he didn't convince **them** (OR **the jury**) that Ms. Scott was guilty.

Pages 74–75

A 1 His explanation that he had been stuck in traffic for over an hour didn't sound right.

2 Their discovery that the boy suffered from asthma changed their attitude.

3 The belief that there are aliens from outer space living among us is very widespread.

B 1 with the view that
2 to the fact that
3 conclusion was (that)
4 against the idea that
5 example of
6 Despite the fact that
7 belief that
8 in agreement that

C 1 premonition ... that ... that
2 Skepticism ... that ... that
3 Superstition ... that ... that
4 Déjà vu ... that ... that

D raise issues how equality can be > issues of (OR about OR with regard to) how
the fact which women don't have > the fact that
based on the belief people's attitudes can be changed > the belief that people's
the assumption other peaceful changes > the assumption that other
in spite of it is largely controlled by men > in spite of the fact that it is

Pages 76–77

A **Par. A:** which sank in 1718 (line 5) OR who was the most notorious pirate of his day (line 6)

Par. B: whose real name was Edward Teach (line 8)

Par. C: when the European powers declared peace (line 15) OR what they knew best (line 19) OR that had the speed and power (line 22) OR which they renamed *Queen Anne's Revenge* (line 25)

Par. D: whose huge black beard was twisted into long tails (line 34) OR who carried several guns and swords in belts (line 35) OR (which were) slung across both shoulders (line 36) OR that he could use (line 38)

Par. E: when he was killed in a sea battle with two British ships (line 41) OR that had been sent (line 42) OR (that) we still have today (line 46)

B
1 whose
2 who
3 that
4 whom
5 that
6 which
7 when
8 that
9 Ø (OR that)

C … all (that) he needed (line 31)
… fuses (that) he could use to ignite cannons during an attack (line 38)

Pages 78–79

A which sank in 1718. (line 5)
which they renamed *Queen Anne's Revenge* (line 25)
Both are non-defining.

B
1 that
2 who
3 which
4 that
5 who
6 who
7 which
8 who
9 that
10 whom

C
1 that uses exaggerated actions, often involving accidents
2 who controls a sporting event
3 in which each competitor takes part in three different sports
4 from whom you rent a room or apartment (OR whom you rent a room or apartment from)
5 , the largest part of which is below the surface of the water,
6 , some of which are poisonous,
7 , which consists of nine islands,
8 , whom most people know as Mark Twain,

D a letter said I had been "terminated." > a letter that said;

the letter, that came from the university, > which; termination (means "the end") > which means; which it felt really weird > which felt; that I could be fired from it > that I could be fired from (OR from which I could be fired); I was just a student didn't have a job > a student who didn't; it was an error had been caused > an error that had; I wasn't the only one had been terminated > the only one who had; A lot of other people didn't have jobs > other people who didn't

Pages 80–81

A
1 If she caught a cold (line 42)
2 if I put a huge swimming pool in front of my house (line 24) OR If I went to all that trouble (line 27) OR If you were in my situation (line 38)

B
1 (Mai-Lei)
2 (Erin)
3 (Anna)
4 (Jamal)
5 (Raina)

C
1 If she has a cup of coffee, she always wants to smoke a cigarette. (line 6) OR If she catches a cold, she goes to bed immediately. (line 50)
2 if she had a cigarette in her hand, she was cool. (line 2)
3 If you are successful, it will be because of hard work. (line 10) OR If you don't experience a struggle, you won't experience the triumph. (line 16) OR If you build it, they will come. (line 22)

D
1 was (f)
2 come (d)
3 is (a)
4 is (e)

5 don't (b)
6 is (c)

Pages 82–83

A
1 if I put a huge swimming pool in front of my house, people would think I was crazy. (line 24) OR If I went to all that trouble, I'd put the pool at the back of my house. (line 27) OR If I were you, I would sell it. (line 30) OR If you were in my situation, I would help you out. (line 38)
2 If he had wanted to sell his car, he would have done that already. (line 33) OR If he had worked harder at school, he would have had some kind of career by now. (lines 36)

B
1 If I knew Jason's phone number, I could tell him what happened.
2 If she had studied for the test, she would (OR could OR might) have passed.
3 If you had warned us about the bad weather, I would (OR could OR might) have brought a toque and mitts.
4 If I was in your situation, I would (OR might) start looking for another job.

C
1 were
2 would start
3 wanted (OR decided)
4 could do
5 started
6 would contribute
7 had started
8 could have paid (OR would have contributed)
9 would have contributed (OR could have paid)
10 decided (OR wanted)
11 would cost
12 would end up

D he always fall asleep > always fell (OR would always fall OR always used to fall);

his feet are near the fire > were;
his slippers start to smoke >
started (OR would start);
my grandmother has to rush
over > had to (OR would
have to);
my father sit in that chair > sits;
he immediately go to sleep
> goes;
and start snoring > starts;
My mother get really annoyed
> gets;
if that happen > happens;
if I take … happen to me >
if I take … will happen (OR
if I took … would happen
OR if I were to take … would
happen);
I don't have this dilemma >
wouldn't;
my older brother didn't move
away > hadn't moved;
If he stays > had stayed;
he is given the chair > would
have been given;
and I am not faced with the
problem > wouldn't be faced
(OR wouldn't have been faced);
If I move > moved;
the chair fit > would (OR
could) fit;
Do I really have a problem
> Would;
if I settle > settled;
and give in > gave;
But who wake me … if my
slippers catch > would wake …
caught (OR will wake … catch)

Pages 84–85

A typical patterns in the
present (1)
the past (2)
to express rules (5)
habits (4)
correlations, such as scientific
observations (3)
when we are explaining how
to do something (6)
for plans (8)
predictions (9)
to ask about future events (11)
to make requests (10)
completely imaginary
situations (14)

potential outcomes of a
course of action (15)
willingness to do something,
despite lack of ability (13)
express regret (17)
assign blame (18)

B 1 (first, 9)
2 (zero, 3)
3 (second, 15)
4 (zero, 5)
5 (third, 16)
6 (zero, 6)
7 (second, 13)
8 (third, 18)

C 1 had asked (c)
2 were (a)
3 don't want (e)
4 hadn't forgotten (b)
5 need (d)

D 1 If that's your goal
2 if the only measure of
success were becoming
a doctor
3 If you tried as hard as
you could
4 If it's complete
5 If not
6 If you've done your best

Pages 86–87

A **Par. A:** so she tried to take
good care of his proud
creation (line 5)
Par. B: Before he began his
career with the national
weather service (line 7) OR
Although he'd had to give up
his artistic ambitions (line 9)
Par. C: because there was
all that cement in the soil
(line 16) OR when he was
mixing the cement, sand,
and water (line 18)
Par. D: When there was a
period of warm summer
weather (line 23) OR Before
Monique could get to them
(line 27)
Par. E: when Monique had
to go out and sweep the
whole country every morning
(line 30) OR If it wasn't wet
(line 32) OR When it rained
a lot (line 35)

Par. F: Even though it wasn't
really cold during most of the
winter (line 38) OR as if it
had been carved from a large
flat slab of marble by an
expert hand (line 44)

B 1 T
2 F
3 F
4 F
5 T
6 T

C 1 After her husband passed
away (line 1)
2 because there was all that
cement in the soil (line 16)
3 When there was a period
of warm summer weather
(line 23)
4 Even though it wasn't
really cold during most
of the winter (line 38)
5 as if it had been carved
from a large flat slab of
marble by an expert hand
(line 44)

Pages 88–89

A 1 When I was standing at
the bus stop in the rain,
I watched Maurice drive
by in his new car.
2 As the skin starts to turn
yellow, you'll know that
the fruit is getting ripe.
3 While we're eating (OR
having OR at) lunch, we
shouldn't talk about
anything to do with work.
4 Just as I was getting out
of the shower, the phone
rang in the other room.

B 1 When
2 When OR While
3 As
4 As OR When OR While

C 1 prediction … before
2 skewer … while
3 postscript … after
4 blender … until

D 1 have been
2 'll be
3 've been

4 'll be
5 will be
6 've been
7 've been
8 will be

Pages 90–91

A 1 (c) as if
2 (a) as
3 (d) as if
4 (b) as

B 1 They all behaved as though nothing had happened.
2 It was still just as I remembered it.
3 It tastes as though it was made yesterday.
4 you try to do as well as they have done.
5 hidden in the forest, just as the guidebook had described it.
6 you think it isn't as much as it really is.

C 1 As it's a holiday, all the banks will be closed on Monday.
2 Since she had an operation on her foot, she has had to use crutches.
3 While we're all together today, we should decide on a date for the barbecue.
4 Now that he has finished his exams, I wonder what he'll do next.

D 1 (c) because
2 (b) as if
3 (a) Because
4 (d) as if

Pages 92–93

A A then (line 7) OR In fact (line 7)
B For example (line 12) OR also (line 15) OR Actually (line 18)
C After all (line 24) OR So (line 25)
D However (line 41) OR As a consequence (line 45)

B 1 (D)
2 (C)

3 (A)
4 (B)

C 1 There are **also** very large signs. (line 14)
2 **What** scientists now believe is that human activity is the cause. (line 28)

Pages 94–95

A 1 As a result of (OR Because of OR As a consequence of)
2 In addition to (OR As well as) … and … as a result (OR as a consequence OR as well OR too).

B 1 in contrast
2 as a result
3 In addition to
4 for example

C 1 also
2 however
3 and
4 but
5 so
6 As a result

D 1 (d) though
2 and (c) So
3 or (a) but
4 (b) So … instead

E in America consequently her English > in America. Consequently, her English (OR in America and consequently her English OR in America, so consequently her English);
She isn't like an American, although > though (OR however);
seem to be very direct, in contrast this Kazuko > seem to be very direct. In contrast, Kazuko (OR seem to be very direct. In contrast to this, Kazuko OR seem to be very direct, but in contrast, Kazuko);
As example > For example;
Instead that > Instead (OR Instead of (doing) that);
She makes also a small > also makes a small;
Alternatively, or she may say >

a small "tsss" sound or she may say (OR a small "tsss" sound. Alternatively, she may say OR a small "tsss" sound. Or she may say)
As a result this > As a result (OR As a result of this)
Nevertheless that > Nevertheless (OR Despite that OR In spite of that)
In other word > In other words

Pages 96–100 (Review test)

The number after each answer indicates the page number on which you can find information about that grammar point.

1 1 a 8
2 d 8
3 a 8
4 b 8

2 1 a 12
2 c 11
3 d 11, 14
4 d 12

3 1 c 14
2 d 14
3 a 14
4 a 14

4 1 b 18
2 b 18
3 d 18
4 d 19

5 1 a 25, 29
2 a 25
3 a 25, 29
4 a 25

6 1 c 32
2 a 32
3 c 32
4 d 34

7 1 d 36
2 a 36
3 b 37
4 d 36

8 1 b 39, 40
2 a 42
3 d 40
4 a 40

9 1 b 58
    2 c 56, 57
    3 d 56
    4 a 56, 57

10 1 b 58, 59
     2 d 55
     3 b 56
     4 a 56, 57

11 1 b 62
     2 b 62
     3 c 62
     4 d 61, 63

12 1 b 74
     2 c 71
     3 d 71
     4 a 72

13 1 b 77
     2 d 77
     3 a 77
     4 b 77

14 1 b 81
     2 b 81
     3 a 81
     4 d 81

15 1 a 88
     2 c 89
     3 c 87
     4 a 99

16 1 a 87, 89
     2 b 87
     3 c 87
     4 c 87

Index

Wed Jan 2nd
Jan 23rd